A Letter TO GOD

The Compelling Testimony of a Life Transformed by an Act of Faith

ANTOINE D. ONGOLO

Xulon PRESS

Copyright © 2014 by Antoine D. Ongolo

A Letter to God
The Compelling Testimony of a Life Transformed by an Act of Faith
by Antoine D. Ongolo

Printed in the United States of America

ISBN 9781629522159

All rights reserved solely by the author. The author guarantees all contents are original and do not infringe upon the legal rights of any other person or work. No part of this book may be reproduced in any form without the permission of the author. The views expressed in this book are not necessarily those of the publisher.

This book is the English translation of *Une lettre à Dieu*. Translated from the French by Ghislain R. Labonté.

Unless otherwise indicated, all quotes from the Bible in this book are from the New King James Version®. Copyright © 1982 by Thomas Nelson, Inc. Used by permission. All rights reserved.

www.xulonpress.com

Dear Bill & Bonnie,

My hope is that this book will renew hope and spark inspiration for whatever challenges you may face. Be blessed!

Antoine

Acknowledgments

I dedicate this book to my mother, my brothers and sisters, and all those who have been to me the cool oasis I needed during my long journey through the desert.

They will know who they are in this true story. However, character names have been changed to protect the privacy of the individuals.

Table of Contents

Chapter 1: Suffering in the Morning of Life 11
Chapter 2: A Life-Changing Event 16
Chapter 3: Discovering My Vocation 25
Chapter 4: Following My Passion. 28
Chapter 5: Hitting Rock Bottom 33
Chapter 6: Spiritual Renewal 38
Chapter 7: The Vision. 43
Chapter 8: Learning Through Faith 48
Chapter 9: Persevering Through Hardships. 54
Chapter 10: Against All Hope. 59
Chapter 11: Faith in Action 64
Chapter 12: At the Crossroads 68
Chapter 13: The Valley of the Shadow of Death 71
Chapter 14: God is Faithful 78
Chapter 15: The Promised Land 83
Chapter 16: Under the Stars. 87
Chapter 17: In the Shelter of the Most High 93
Chapter 18: Between the Hammer and the Anvil 97
Chapter 19: Face To Face 103
Chapter 20: The Hour of Truth 106
Chapter 21: The Fullness of the Blessing 112
Epilogue. 123

Psalm 23

The LORD is my shepherd;
I shall not want.
He makes me to lie down in green pastures;
He leads me beside the still waters.
He restores my soul;
He leads me in the paths of righteousness
For His name's sake.
Yea, though I walk through the valley of the shadow of death,
I will fear no evil;
For You are with me;
Your rod and Your staff, they comfort me.
You prepare a table before me in the presence of my enemies;
You anoint my head with oil;
My cup runs over.
Surely goodness and mercy shall follow me
All the days of my life;
And I will dwell in the house of the LORD
Forever.

CHAPTER 1

Suffering in the Morning of Life

*"A father of the fatherless, a defender of widows,
Is God in His holy habitation." (Psalm 68:5)*

I came into the world on a bright starry night of August 1980, in Yaoundé, the capital of Cameroon. My father was a former soldier who had become a bank employee. He held the position of staff representative in one of the country's most prestigious banks. My mother was a housewife. We were seven children born from the same womb: four girls and three boys. I occupy the third rank among my siblings, considering only my mother's children. Yes, my father was a polygamist. He already had six children with a first wife when he married my mother. We were thirteen children living on the same property.

The family home was located in the popular Etoudi district, north of Yaoundé. Dad had built two houses side by side in the same enclosure: one for his first wife and her children, and the other for my mother and her children. The arrangement seemed to work perfectly. As a good military man, Dad knew the proper strategies that would preserve the peace between his two wives. As far as I can remember, no major conflict ever rose between them while Father was living. Due to his intelligence and financial position, he had managed to build a large family. We were happy and united... until April 10, 1990.

That day, as usual, my brothers and I were all gone to school. We attended the French public school of Bastos, listed among the most esteemed schools in the capital. I was in my fifth year, the year before last of primary school.[1] During the noon break, a few people from my family arrived at school and took us home in emergency. As soon as I noticed that a stranger was driving my father's white Peugeot 504, I knew instantly that something serious had happened... something very serious!

Dad had been suffering of a critical illness for some time. In fact, the doctors had told him that his days were numbered. A few days before that sudden appearance of family members at school, Dad had decided to visit his village about 40 miles from Yaoundé, probably to bid farewell to his native land. My childhood carelessness prevented me from worrying. I never thought the situation was so serious. However, on that famous April 10th, I had to face reality: Dad had died.

Life for my family took a completely different turn after this tragic event, the second in the space of two years. My father's younger brother had lost his life two years earlier. He was a doctor living with his wife and nine children in a small town in southern Cameroon. After my uncle's death, Father took it upon himself to take care of my aunt and her nine children, inviting them to live with us. I don't know how he did it, but the fact remains that he managed to feed and ensure the schooling of 22 children. These additional responsibilities on my father's shoulders did not even affect

---

[1] Education in Cameroon follows the French system in which primary school includes kindergarten plus five grades at the elementary level. The fifth grade then corresponds to the same level in the U.S. education system, though it might be called the last year of elementary school or the first year of middle school, depending on the state or school district.

our quality of life in any significant manner, apart from the fact that we had to share our bedrooms with our cousins.

After Dad's death, our daily life became a nightmare. Three unemployed widows had now the responsibility of raising twenty-two children. The pension received from the National Social Security Fund[2] was evidently insufficient to properly feed so many hungry stomachs. In the evening, when my brothers and I returned home from school after an hour-long walk, we knew more or less what dinner would include. Couscous was cheap then. We ate it just about everyday. I had enough of couscous. I longed for a more balanced and varied diet, but the three widows' purchasing power was very limited.

For the meals, the household was divided into five groups according to age and sex: mothers, young women, girls, young men and boys. I was ten years old at the time; I belonged to the last group. We were six boys crowded around one plate. There was so little to eat that everyone had better be well prepared for battle, and the boys made no bones about their stance: the goal was to eat faster than the next one. Since we did not fight on equal terms in this jungle, one of my cousins, the dean of the group, found a trick as unusual as effective to make sure the portions were equal.

He set up a monitoring system through which each boy filled his spoon, and then waited till my cousin checked the quantity of food in each spoon. He made sure the amount was the same for all; otherwise, the surplus had to be returned to the plate. In such a case, the dean of the group proceeded to a second check before giving the green light to take the spoon to the mouth. And the cycle was repeated until the plate was emptied.

As time went by, the coexistence of the three widows became more fragile. To keep the peace, it was decided

---

[2] In French: Caisse nationale de prévoyance sociale, CNPS.

that each widow would take care of her own children. Aunt Helen, my uncle's widow, left the house; my half-brothers and their mother occupied a part of the family compound, and my mother with my brothers and sisters, we occupied another part. My mother devoted herself wholeheartedly to raise us in the best possible way. Any business she could get her hands on was an opportunity to be seized. She bought and sold food products at times; she managed a cafeteria other times. She really did her best to feed us, and she succeeded.

I ended up getting used to suffering. One of the most difficult moments remained the wake-up call by my mother in the early morning, precisely when sleep is the most comfortable. "Get up," she yelled. "It's time to fetch water and to get ready for school." A fifteen-minute walk led to the well. Every morning, a huge crowd from the surrounding area gathered around it. To avoid losing time in the lineup, one had to get there before daybreak.

I usually walked to the well still dozing and trying hard to return to the dream so brutally interrupted by Mom's call. But the rough path brought me back to reality very quickly. The last part of the path ended in a slippery downward slope covered with bushes. I had to be extra vigilant. Coming back up revealed still more risky. With a four-gallon bucket on my head, my balance was jeopardized at every step. Indeed, I did slip and fall several times. In such circumstances, I casually turned around and sadly took my place in the queue, well aware that in a few hours, life would be rough at school.

I was an average pupil in primary school. I loved Mrs. Onana, my teacher in sixth grade. She did not compare at all with the mean teacher I had in fifth grade. That one used to whip me every time I was late. Could he not understand that I was a little orphan who had to fetch water from the well every morning before walking to school? He never tried to understand why I often arrived late, but he found an easy solution to my problem: the whip.

Mrs. Onana was different. She was very kind to me and gave me her full attention. I became a much better pupil because of her gentleness. She often asked me to read to the class. One of my favorite stories was an excerpt from the book *Cruel City* by the Cameroonian author Eza Boto.[3] I still remember parts of the story:

> *I love my mother. Ooh! I love her like you cannot imagine. [...] When my father died, I was only a few years old. My mother took on the task of raising me. She was extremely attentive. [...] I was better dressed than the boys of my age who still had their father.*

At the end of my reading, I shed a few tears sometimes. Mrs. Onana must have known that the story was talking about me, about my life, Mom and my love for her... As for my classmates, they had no idea of the tie that bound me to that story. For them, it was just another story.

That year, I finished primary school[4] with excellent grades.

---

3   In French: *Ville cruelle*.
4   Grade 6 in the U.S. education system.

Chapter 2

A Life-Changing Event

*"Remember now your Creator in the days of
your youth,
Before the difficult days come,
And the years draw near when you say,
I have no pleasure in them." (Ecclesiastes 12:1)*

Mfou was about ten miles away from Yaoundé. It was a quiet town where life was good. Our house stood right in the city center. Uncle Nestor, my maternal aunt's husband, held the position of postmaster, and his official residence was connected to the post office. He had agreed to support me after primary school.[5] That was a relief for Mom, whose burden was somewhat lightened, and a godsend for me, because life with my aunt, uncle and cousins was much easier than what I had known with the crowd of orphans in Yaoundé. I would finally be able to eat normally, go to school normally... in short, live like a normal child.

---

5   In the French education system, primary school is followed by secondary school called *collège* for the first four grades (6th, 5th, 4th, 3rd) and *lycée* for the last three grades (2nd, 1st, *terminale*). In Cameroon, all grades of secondary school are referred to as the *lycée*. In both systems, the baccalaureate is the degree granted after the *terminale*.

A Life-Changing Event

My aunt had five children when I arrived in the household. She took me in one hundred percent, gave me the love and care an orphan needs, never discriminating between her own children and me. So, the beginning of my teenage years was relatively peaceful. I learned to live with my cousins as I had lived with my brothers and sisters. Sometimes I felt like I was not quite at home, but how could it have been otherwise? One never has more than one home really, which is always missed, however welcoming another family can be...

Every Sunday, my aunt took us to a church in the neighborhood. The same fervor was displayed each time: worship bathed in such an atmosphere of praise and adoration that I could feel God's presence inside and all around me. The children of my age gathered in a separate room for Sunday school. We were taught that Jesus Christ loves us, and that He showed it by dying on the cross to set us free from sin and reconcile us with God.[6]

After a year, I was forced to give up Sunday school because of family conflicts. However, one thing remained: the teaching I had received had left an indelible impression on my heart. Even away from the church, I knew that the seed had been planted: the word of God would sprout sooner or later.[7]

Sunday school out, I was left with regular school. I was in sixth class, the first year at the *lycée* in Mfou. My grades were not great. I had always been an average student. It was no reason to be concerned really, except for certain disciplines that did need the alarm bell to be set off: such was the case for French.

I will never forget the event! Mr. Lobé, the French teacher, was about to hand out the copies of a composition

---

[6] "For God so loved the world that He gave His only begotten Son, that whoever believes in Him should not perish but have everlasting life." (John 3:16)

[7] "Train up a child in the way he should go, And when he is old he will not depart from it." (Proverbs 22:6)

the students had written a few days earlier. Straightaway, he announced that he would read one of them that shined by its mediocrity. The students looked at each other, worried. Whose writing could be so bad that the teacher would display it as an example not to follow? The wait became unbearable. Mr. Lobé spoke a name... mine!

My paper was full of grammatical and spelling errors, of nonsense, besides being completely off-topic. As my classmates booed, the teacher blithely continued reading. The moment was an ordeal for me; I felt violated in my dignity and my honor. I had become the moron of the French class, a dirty label that I certainly did not want to keep.

I decided that this was not going to happen again, and the following school year, I increased my efforts in French. Grammar books became my friends; I got familiar with all grammar rules. In fourth grade,[8] I committed to read more. Every week I borrowed books from the school library. As my passion for reading grew, so did my knowledge of French.

In 1995, in third grade,[9] I was surprised to face Mr. Lobé, the teacher who had so profoundly humiliated me three years earlier. He was going to teach me French again. I was rather proud, actually, because soon he would find out that a lot of water had flowed under the bridge since he had exposed my shortcomings as a writer.

At the end of the school year, as usual, Mr. Lobé decided to read a paper to the class, but not one he considered an example to shun, as he had done three years earlier, but one he presented as a model to be imitated. The paper was so well written that Mr. Lobé could not refrain from reading it to all the students. Who was this brilliant writer? The tension in

---

8   This is the third year at the *lycée*. The equivalent is the first year of high school in the U.S., freshman level. From now on, the author will use the USA education system equivalents in the text itself instead of providing them in the footnotes.

9   Sophomore level.

A Life-Changing Event

class became tangible; the teacher spoke a name...mine! Of course, I received congratulations from all the students. In the space of three years, I had vindicated my honor, moving up from the last to the first rank.

In 1997, I had become a lank adolescent of seventeen years old. Five years had gone by since I had stopped going to church. My life was very much like any young person's life of my age. I was in high school, and tried to conform to the fashion of the time to appeal to girls. At the same time, I had concerns of a totally different nature: I was desperately seeking God. I was eager to learn more about God, his identity and his true church. I began to watch television programs discussing religion, hoping to find the path leading to God. However, the number of religious dogmas confused me.

I then remembered the spiritual fervor I had felt in the church I had attended five years earlier. I also remembered what I had learned at Sunday school about Jesus Christ being the way, the truth and the life, and that nobody can go to the Father except through Him.[10] At the time, I was much too young to understand the true meaning of these words, but some time had elapsed since then, and now I understood the thrust of their message. As I meditated on it, I became convinced in my heart that I had to accept Jesus Christ in my life as my Lord and personal Savior.[11]

Yet, I did not feel ready to commit to that path, not due to of a lack of conviction, but because I was prejudiced against Christians and their way of life in general. I thought that being a Christian meant that I would have to commit to a life of devotion, famine and poverty, a spiritual life devoid of prosperity and glamor, too serious for the young man I was. I yearned to have fun and many friends in my life. I did not want to look like those Christians who were poorly

---

10   John 14:6
11   "If you confess with your mouth the Lord Jesus and believe in your heart that God has raised Him from the dead, you will be saved." (Romans 10:9)

dressed, unconcerned about their physical appearance and completely out of touch with the world.

I was a very ambitious teenager. I intended to make the most of my promising intellect and my talents. Why would I confine myself to a monotonous life that did not emphasize my worth? So I decided to postpone my Christian commitment. I would first enjoy my youth, have the career of my dreams and gain the international notoriety I aspired to. In short, I would live my life. Only later, perhaps at fifty or sixty years old, I would adopt the Christian life and ask Jesus Christ to be my old-age companion.

But Jesus Christ gave his life in his prime, at the age of thirty-three. He did not wait to be old to offer his life in sacrifice on the cross because of our sins.[12] As for me, born a sinner after the fall of Adam, I was condemned to spend eternity in hell, cut off from God forever. But God Eternal, in his infinite love for me and for humanity, gave his only begotten Son, that whosoever believes in Him should not perish, but have everlasting life.

I knew those truths I had learned in Sunday school, but I did not want to stifle my youth. God saw my attitude, and found a strategy to make me reconsider my decision. One day in March, a group of Christians from Yaoundé organized a Gospel crusade in Mfou. It took place on the terrace next to the event hall across the street from our house. It was not the first time an event of that nature was presented there. I attended all the sessions; I was keen to hear the Good News of Jesus Christ, yet careful not to let them indoctrinate me.

That day, however, my prejudices were hacked, one after the other. The crusade was conducted by a group of Christians of my age. They all belonged to the same group, the Young Harvesters for Christ.[13] Their commitment to the

---

12 "For the wages of sin is death, but the gift of God is eternal life in Christ Jesus our Lord." (Romans 6:23)
13 In French: *Les jeunes moissonneurs pour Christ*.

Lord's work surprised me: they were so beautiful, so happy, obviously fulfilled in their Christian life. The sketches, poems, quiz, music, dance and exhortation made me realize that their talents were perfectly expressed in the house of God. And they were not a poverty-stricken group. From their appearance, I could see that they belonged to a social class well above mine. Christian life was not only for the poor! Even the rich could serve God...

I was in the presence of young people like me who were intelligent, talented, came from wealthy families and, above all, they loved Jesus Christ. They had all the qualities that I thought were incompatible with Christian living, yet they had chosen to serve God in their youth. I saw that their life was not boring, sad or lonely. On the opposite, it was abundant. As a child of the Most High, I could aspire to prosperity and to a quality education, to an influential position in my country and even internationally. That day, I realized that God needs intelligent and educated Christians who have influence, and will let the light of Christ shine in the world.[14]

The transformation and renewal process of my intelligence had just been triggered. The day after the Gospel crusade, I went to the campsite where the Young Harvesters for Christ had taken refuge for their spiritual retreat. It was the last day before they returned to Yaoundé. I let them know that I wanted to serve the Lord and belong to Him. They called two leaders, who led me in the prayer of repentance. No sooner had I finished the prayer that I felt light and deeply happy. It was as if a very heavy burden had just been lifted off my shoulders. I was filled with an indescribable sense of well-being, heightened by a deep feeling of safety. Without a doubt, He had come into my heart to make me a new creature.

---

14   "Let your light so shine before men, that they may see your good works and glorify your Father in heaven." (Matthew 5:16)

Shortly after, the Young Harvesters for Christ decided to parade through the city as their final opportunity to celebrate the Lord's name through the streets of Mfou. I was terrified at the thought of parading in this town where everyone knew each other. I wanted to decline the invitation, but one of the youth had a strong argument against it: "If you are ashamed of Jesus before men," he said, "Jesus will be ashamed of you before his Father on the day of judgment." His logic was all the more relevant since my conversion had taken place in private. The day before, during the Gospel crusade, I had not wanted to be seen in public. If anything, God himself was orchestrating this walk so that I would present my new identity in Christ to the entire city.

After the walk, we returned to the campsite, happy to have set the streets burning with the fire of praise. The evening began with a reports session. The opportunity was given to every youth to witness of the wonders that God had made in his life during this spiritual retreat. I had so much to say, but my shyness kept me glued to my seat, unable to lift a finger. As the evening drew to a close, I realized that it was now or never. The Spirit of God, who had just recently come to make his home in me, gave me the strength to overcome my shyness.[15] Thus, the day of my conversion became the day when I spoke in public for the fist time.

This, in itself, was a small miracle; I was the epitome of shyness. Even more interesting still, I discovered that I had an unsuspected talent for public speaking. My introductory statement set off a thunder of applause in the room: "I am called Antoine, but as of this morning, they call me brother Antoine..." What a beautiful formulation to announce my change of status in Jesus Christ! The public was riveted, in admiration. It gave me the courage to exhibit my most beautiful prose with confidence. At seventeen, on the day of

---

15   "For God has not given us a spirit of fear, but of power and of love and of a sound mind." (2 Timothy 1:7)

my conversion, the Lord had given me an oratorical talent, or perhaps revealed a talent I already had. And to think that only a few days earlier, I had been hesitant to entrust my youth to Jesus Christ for fear of not being able to develop my talents...

Come Monday morning, I went back to school after that weekend of renewal. To my surprise, I discovered that my classmates had been plotting against me. "We saw you Saturday singing and dancing in the street with a group of people..." Many were ironic and sarcastic in their questioning, surprised by my choice to serve the Lord in my youth. Far from upsetting me, their snide remarks rather reinforced my belief in the authenticity of my conversion. Not only had I confessed Jesus Christ, but I had done it publicly before the entire city.[16]

One year had passed since I had accepted the Lord in my life. I was now in my last year of high school. It was an especially difficult year for me. One day, returning from school, I was shocked by the discovery that my room had been broken into. The thieves had taken all the books and textbooks that my mother had bought for me. They had also stolen my new pair of sneakers, purchased for that school year.

So I began my year feeling down in the dumps. For several weeks, I had to go to school in sandals and during all that year, I did not manage to replace the stolen books. My grades were catastrophic. Clearly, I was heading for a failure. I would not get my high school diploma. But God decided otherwise...

One week before the exit exam, Simon, my neighbor in class and my best friend, lent me two booklets on exit exams used in another state in years past, with questions in math and chemistry. I had only one week to prepare for the exam.

---

[16] "Therefore whoever confesses Me before men, him I will also confess before My Father who is in heaven. But whoever denies Me before men, him I will also deny before My Father who is in heaven." (Matthew 10:32-33)

I randomly selected three questions in mathematics, among the many in the booklet, and I did the same for chemistry.

What a surprise, on the day of the exam, to discover that two of the three questions in the mathematics section were among the ones that I had studied in the booklet! Mere coincidence? That's what I thought at first, except that the chemistry section also had two questions that I had randomly studied in the booklet. In both cases, the exam presented the exact same questions that I had studied two days earlier, commas included.

Someone had to be behind this incident. I looked around; only one person in my circle of friends[17] was capable of such a thing; that was God. He had seen my tears and my sorrow, following the theft of my schoolbooks. Though I did not deserve to get the diploma, God, in his majesty, decided to come to my rescue, and grant me the help I needed to succeed.

---

17   "No longer do I call you servants, for a servant does not know what his master is doing; but I have called you friends, for all things that I heard from My Father I have made known to you." (John 15:15)

CHAPTER 3

Discovering My Vocation

"I [...] beseech you to walk worthy of the calling with which you were called." (Ephesians 4:1)

I was curious when I crossed the threshold of the radio station in Yaoundé on Thursday, July 16, 1998. Indeed, a few days earlier, Cameroon's National Radio had launched a call for budding journalists. As part of a summer program, internships were offered to youth attracted to journalism. I was bored that summer, so I showed up at the audition with the sole purpose of discovering the world of radio. Dozens of young people were present at the audition, with only a few positions to be filled. I felt intimidated among my competitors in the waiting room: for the most part, they were students from the University of Yaoundé. I was eighteen years old, not even registered at the university. I had just obtained my high school diploma.

The recruiters led us into a large room where the audition was held. The test consisted in writing an article on a current topic of our choice, and then to read it to a jury. I chose to write on the celebration of the anniversary of the storming of the Bastille; it had taken place two days earlier, on July 14th. When I finished reading my article in front of the jury, I felt something I would call a journalistic twinge. The relevance of the text and the quality of the reading both surprised me. My voice was warm, broadcast quality... I noticed that the jury had been seduced by my voice. That day, I discovered that I had a real oratorical talent; it took me back to the witness I had given on the evening of my conversion to Jesus Christ. I was outstanding among the young people who were recruited by the radio station. Through reports, interviews and time on air, I quickly learned to master the basics of journalism. I became passionate about it. I did not need more convincing: I was cut out for that work. Yet, I chose not to apply at the Graduate School of Journalism in Cameroon. I enrolled instead at the Faculty of Economics and Management at the University of Yaoundé. My father's profession might have influenced me, unconsciously wishing to become a banker like him. I'm not sure. Passion for journalism did consume me, and I knew it was the career of my dreams. Since I was already registered in economics, why not become a financial journalist?

My first year in university went quite normally. I was admitted to the second year without a problem, but unfortunately, I could not finish it because of financial hardships. In early 2000, the National Social Security Fund withheld my mother's pension because of a family dispute. The household was thus left without any means of subsistence. The consequences were dramatic for my brothers and me, especially in regards to our schooling.

Since we were not in school anymore, my little brother and I began selling bread to support the family. Every morning, we picked up bread at a bakery in Etoudi, our home neighborhood, and sold it in the Mokolo market, one of the largest markets in Yaoundé. Daily profits were meager, but still, they helped in our misery. We were so pitiful that a simple meal at home had almost become a luxury. We ate at home two to three times a week. For the rest of the time, we were all left on our own.

Discovering My Vocation

My way to ensure my meals was to visit my friend Alain everyday at the fire station. I made sure I arrived at 1:00 P.M. sharp, lunch hour. Alain never asked me why my visits were so frequent and always at the same time. I am sure he suspected that hunger was my main motivation. The other firefighters did not raise any objection about sharing their meal. They got used to my presence.

It's also because of hunger that I visited more frequently the family of the two high school teenagers I was tutoring. I was paid a small salary for three sessions a week, but I went four and five times each week because the family served me a hearty meal after each session. The parents were grateful for my generosity. Indeed, I devoted more time to their children without asking anything in return. They did not realize that each additional hour I offered was actually paid in kind by the food they gave me.

In October 2000, I felt the need for a change of scenery. I was fed up with that life, fed up with the same things around me, fed up with Yaoundé. So I took advantage of the visit of an uncle to ask him if I could go live with him. He worked in Douala, a commercial city and the main door to Cameroon. After a few days, my uncle called me: "Yes, you can come to Douala to continue your education..."

CHAPTER 4

Following My Passion

"He has made everything beautiful in its time..."
(Ecclesiastes 3:11)

I absolutely had no doubt now: a career in journalism was tailor-made for me. My performance in front of the youth group of my church in the summer of 2001 constituted clear evidence. I had gathered a team of four people, and each morning, we presented news on the radio about the highlights of the camp. Our broadcasts covered the spiritual nature of the retreat as well as its festive aspects and general news. I was the instigator of this project; it had never been tried before in such a context. Success was instantaneous and, very quickly, I became an icon for the youth of my church, who acknowledged that I had a real talent for journalism.

Beyond the fame acquired through the camp radio news, I enjoyed a visit from God during that retreat week. The preacher had hammered at the pulpit: "I have been crucified with Christ; it is no longer I who live, but Christ lives in me..."[18] At twenty-one years old, I did not understand the full meaning of this message, but one thing is certain: I chose

---

18   Galatians 2:20.

to surrender to Jesus' loving arms.[19] Besides, it was in my best interest; I needed a power greater than mine to break the stalemate that I was in.

I had decided to leave my uncle's house just before the retreat. I wanted to live my Christian faith in peace, without having to present any justification. However, I did not know where to go. The spiritual retreat for the youth of the church had offered a perfect transition. Now though, as the retreat was over, I had to find a place to stay. I approached Sebastian, a Christian friend from my church. Without much hesitation, he agreed to take me in.

Sebastian lived close to the University of Douala; this proximity was a blessing for me, because I did not have to travel long distance anymore to get there, as had been the case when I lived with my uncle. He had welcomed me when I had arrived in this city. Thanks to him, I had been able to resume my studies at the Faculty of Economics and Management of the University of Douala. I was in my second year.

Although I was determined to continue my studies in economics and management, I realized at mid-term that I did not want to make a career in that field. In fact, instead of studying for classes, I spent my time writing articles for the university newspaper. So I decided to change course, and to enroll in social communication. Several friends and relatives thought my decision to drop out was irrational: two years down the drain. I was convinced, however, that this was the right path for me. Had not the youth group recently confirmed that I was cut out for journalism and communication? *It is never too late to follow one's passion*, I thought, *even if it means starting from scratch.*

Life at Sebastian's apartment was not easy. We did not have sufficient money to meet the needs of the household.

---

[19] "For You are my hope, O Lord GOD; You are my trust from my youth." (Psalms 71:5)

He did not have a stable job, and I had none. I gave a few irregular tutoring classes to high school students, but the pay was insignificant. My family in Yaoundé could not help either. They probably were worse off than I was.

I was begging to the shopkeeper in the neighborhood when I had nothing to eat. On a lucky day, he gave me stale bread that I dipped in sugar water; it provided the strength I needed to go to my classes. I should not have left my uncle's house. At least I ate my fill at his place. After talking it over with Sebastian, I started looking for another place to stay.

I called upon David, one of my mother's younger brothers. As a temporary solution, he found a student room for me close to his home in Douala. A few months later, I went to live with him. He was living at Robert's place, one of his best friends who kindly accepted me in his two-bedroom apartment, one for Robert and his girlfriend, one for my uncle and me. In this new environment, I got ready to face the professional world.

In March 2002, a new radio station in Douala opened an audition for journalists and presenters. I mentioned it to Nicole, a close friend I considered talented for this kind of work, and we went together. The prospect of working at that radio station made me very happy! I put all my hopes in that audition; God had answered my prayers. Finally, I'd pull out of poverty and earn some money, even if modestly. Furthermore, the thought of receiving an income in the near future made me reconsider the value of school. I harbored the intention of stopping my studies in communication as soon as I signed my contract with the radio station. Before the start of the audition, I prayed to God again not to let me down when I was in such a critical need of his help.

God let me down! At least, that's what I felt. He did not heed my request, and my application was rejected. My name was not even included on the reserve list, as was the case for Nicole. I was eager to wake up from this nightmare, because

I could not get used to the idea that I had been rejected, me, so brilliant, so talented, born for this job. I did not sleep at all that night. Why had God not helped me? Did He not see my suffering? Did He not understand that I was tired of going to the university on foot every day?

In any event, I had to accept reality. If I could not work at the radio station, I had to pursue my university studies. Despite the pain and discouragement, I completed the first year successfully and moved on to the second year in communication. At this point though, my mindset underwent an extraordinary metamorphosis: I committed to my studies with a firm desire to succeed, to reach as high as I possibly could. Nothing would stop me, not even a journalist's position in a radio station.

A few months after that famous failed audition, a group of students from the University of Douala had the ingenious idea of creating a club to support the activities of the radio station. Station officials gave them airtime to show their support for the campus radio. The club president was a friend well aware of my passion for journalism; he asked me to be a radio host. So, here I was in the studios of the radio station whose doors had been closed to me a few months earlier.

My performance was noted; the director himself made a special visit to the studio to congratulate me. He had been listening to the broadcast at home, and had not been able to resist a trip to the station in search of this young man, whose voice left no one indifferent. How could he not have noticed that voice at the audition? If at all possible, God himself had planned it all.

A few weeks later, I began an internship at that radio station. No longer did I think of interrupting my studies. I was working halftime and going to school halftime. God had just given me a job at the radio station, for which I had shed so many tears. I understood that He had not let me down. He makes everything beautiful in his time, and his time is the best.[20] Indeed, had I been successful at the audition, I would have abandoned my studies. Seeing this attitude in my heart, God had not allowed that I be recruited when I wanted to be, because He wanted to protect my future by keeping me in school.

In 2004, I obtained my degree in communication. At the same time, I was confirmed as a radio journalist. Thus, the audition that had seemed a failure at first revealed to be a saving grace a few months later. I blessed God for his perfect timing: had I obtained that position in 2002, I probably would never have known the wonderful feeling of obtaining a degree in communication. More seriously, I certainly would not have progressed in this profession that requires a high level of knowledge.

The desired fruits of that progress ripened in June 2005. After three years in radio, I yearned for a new challenge. Fortunately, a private television network had just been launched in Douala. I put in my application, and got the position of journalist and reporter. Thus began a new adventure.

---

20   "He has made everything beautiful in its time..." (Ecclesiastes 3:11)

CHAPTER 5

Hitting Rock Bottom

*"Unless the Lord builds the house,
They labor in vain who build it; ..."
(Psalms 127:1)*

The beginning of the year was like no other. Of course, a celebratory atmosphere prevailed on this first day of the year 2009. The New Year's celebrations were a happy event for many. People exchanged best wishes. Unfortunately, I was not in the mood, nor was I looking forward to a day of songs ahead, as is the custom at the dawn of a new year. No matter how hard I tried to be optimistic, it was to no avail: my soul and spirit were wounded, unable to look to the future with confidence. I was finally understanding the popular adage: *hope springs eternal*. Nothing nourished any eternal hope in my despair; on the contrary, it was leading to a slow death. How could the sun have stopped illuminating my world once teeming with new ideas, and enlivened with such creativity? The question haunted me; I could not concentrate on my work.

I had been working as a journalist in a private television station for four years now. My climb up the ladder in the organization had been meteoric. In the first year and a half, I had moved from a simple reporter to the anchor of the evening news program, a great reward for my skills that had not taken long to show. I had been sent all over Cameroon to report on political, economic, social, cultural and even sports events. In addition, I had hosted different television shows on various topics. My talent was recognized, and I was respected among my peers.

However, as we welcomed the New Year, the flame of journalism was beginning to dwindle. I had the impression that I had covered it all. The motivation was gone. On the outside, I still projected the image of a brilliant journalist, but on the inside, I was moaning over my fate. After the failure of all my projects during the previous year, I really thought that I was in the twilight of my career.

That year was supposed to be the best year of my life. I had planned it such without consulting God. On a personal level, I had intended to get married that year. On a professional level, I had taken a number of actions to give my career a boost. I had actually participated in four competitions set up to reward journalistic merit. Three of the competitions had an international reach, while the fourth offered recognition within Cameroon. I was confident that I would strike gold: I would definitely win at least one contest in my group; I was way too smart—in my eyes—to miss out on these opportunities.

One of the international competitions required the production of a report on a given topic. The top four reports would be rewarded, and the winners would be granted a work-related stay in Europe. In the event that I won, I was determined to make, of my time in Europe, an occasion to give a new impetus to my career. I would produce reports on major topics of the economy, and then would become a recognized economic journalist, all according to my plan.

On the day of the announcement of the results, I traveled to Yaoundé, certain that I would figure among the winners. First, the jury proclaimed the top ten finalists. My report was on the list. Then, the jury unveiled the first-prize winner, the second-prize winner, and... no more! Initially, four reports were supposed to be rewarded. Why had this number been reduced to two? The organizing committee did not provide a convincing answer. Could it be that I had ranked third or fourth? I will probably never know. The prize in which I had invested so much had passed me by.

As it never rains but it pours, I won neither the other two contests with an international aspect, nor the local competition. In my quest for fame, I was really hoping to win at least the local contest. The deal was over! In 2008, I was very far from having reached the professional heights I was dreaming of.

My downfall was not restricted to my professional life. My love life, at the end of that same year, also experienced one of the darkest episodes in its history. I was in love with Rosita. We had met at church; for a year, we had spoken the verb love, at times in the indicative of happiness, at times in the conditional of challenges. Our many arguments did cast doubt on a common future. Finally, I came to the conclusion that we were not made to live together. The break was very painful...

That double failure in my personal and professional life really left me in a sorry state. Year 2009 thus began inauspiciously. All hope was destroyed. The journalism work I used to adore did not provide any pleasure anymore. I had to beat myself to show up at work. Tired of pretending, I took a break to rest from the fruitless efforts of the previous year.

I chose the family home in Yaoundé to give me that respite. It was in February. Mother suggested that I accompany her to a church where a young prophet of God was apparently doing wonders. My heart was not leaning towards God at all. On the opposite, I was angry with Him for having let 2008, a year for which I had such high hopes, become so distressful.

A Letter to God

Besides, I had not entered a church for a long time, but my mother proved convincing; I agreed to go with her.

The young prophet's name was Daniel. He was barely eighteen years old. How could one declare himself a prophet of the Lord at that age? The question had remained a whisper within, but God knows our thoughts and probes our hearts.[21] Toward the end of the prayer session, the young man made a startling statement: "Someone in this room is here for the first time. That person is devastated, discouraged, and has lost all hope in life. The Lord asks me to tell that person that there is still hope. God has a glorious future in store for that person." I did not need a divine revelation to understand that these words were about me. Such a thing had never happened in my life before. Of course, as a Christian, I had often heard prophets say things about people, but I took it cautiously, never totally convinced that it all came from God. But this time, it was about me. God had revealed a part of my life to this young man, whom I had underestimated in my heart.

At the end of the session, I introduced myself to the prophet[22] and told him about my despair. He confirmed that God would not only lift me up, but also make me a person of influence in the world. My dreams of greatness came back to life, this time with Jesus Christ as the main actor in the vision. I had tried to do it all by myself, relying on my intelligence, but the failure had been bitter. I had just understood that as long as I believed myself capable of leading my life, according to my will, God would simply watch me do it. Now that I had hit rock bottom, and realized that I could absolutely not succeed on my own, God would take over.[23] I even wondered if God Himself had not prevented the

---

21   "O Lord, You have searched me and known *me*." (Psalms 139:1)
22   "...Believe in the Lord your God, and you shall be established; believe His prophets, and you shall prosper." (2 Chronicles 20:20)
23   "Not that we are sufficient of ourselves to think of anything as being from ourselves, but our sufficiency is from God." (2 Corinthians 3:5)

success of my professional ambitions so that I would realize that whoever builds his future without Him builds in vain.

Another day, the prophet Daniel, talking about me, spoke these words: "Africa, Africa, Africa, Europe, Europe, Europe." When I asked him what that meant, he told me that the Lord would lead me to several African countries and Europe. This was obviously good news, given the despair in which I was immersed. The sun was shining again; there was hope for my life.

I returned to work in Douala, spiritually renewed. A few weeks later, the director of a communications firm in Cotonou, Benin contacted me. He had noticed my professionalism during a trip that I had made a few months earlier in his country, in the context of an international forum. This director asked me to work with him on a sub-regional project that required that I move to Cotonou.

When I accepted the proposal, the words of the young prophet came to mind: "Africa, Africa." So the prophecy was accurate then.

CHAPTER 6

Spiritual Renewal

*"Your word is a lamp to my feet
And a light to my path."
(Psalms 119:105)*

For a while now, I had been looking for a place of worship in Cotonou. I did not feel at home in the two churches I had visited. As I pondered on the subject, I remembered that something had caught my attention when I was staying at the hotel on my arrival in this city. I was out for a walk in the neighborhood, and while I was walking along a shopping street, I heard songs of praise and adoration from a building. I had been delighted; still, I had not stopped. A month later, the memory of these Christian melodies seemed to show me the path. I decided to visit that church to check it out.

As I crossed the threshold of Action Faith Church, I felt a profound joy in my soul. Somehow, I knew I had landed in the right place where God wanted me. The choir was grandiose! It seemed to be divinely anointed, so sublime it was. I had never experienced singing like that before. Besides, I'll never forget the song that greeted me on that first visit: "Lord, I am lost without you, I am desperate for you." I knelt before God in adoration under the power of this vocal piece that had such an effect on me. That day, I gave the Lord an offering of $10.00 (5,000 FCFA[24]), ten times the amount I used to give at my church in Cameroon. Clearly, the transformation process of my heart had begun.

The church was about to organize a major conference of prayer and adoration for mid-July 2009. I was hoping to attend, but my work schedule would not allow me. My boss, Jean-Paul, had scheduled shootings at the same time. We were going to Togo, Ghana, Burkina Faso and the Ivory Coast. We had planned to meet with senior officials of banks and institutions in each country to discuss various topics related to the stock market and to investments. However, before the beginning of this trip, something unusual occurred.

All means of communication at the firm shut down, one after the other. The telephone line went dead; the fax did not work properly. And as if that were not enough, the Internet connection also gave up. Obviously, the preparation of our sub-regional tour was affected. We were no longer able to communicate with our partners in other countries. Therefore, Jean-Paul decided to postpone the shootings. I received the news with a mixture of sadness and joy: the sadness of postponing a tour that I was eager to start, and the joy of being free to attend the conference at my church.

The conference began in mid-July as planned. For one week, pastors, evangelists and prophets from several African countries ignited the audience with fiery sermons. The whole week turned out to be one deep communion experience with God for me. I had never experienced a Christian crusade with such intensity. I was convinced in my mind that the Lord Himself had orchestrated the disruption of communication in the firm to allow me to attend. Not only did the crusade trigger a spiritual awakening for me, it opened a new path in my walk with God.

---

24   FCFA: *Franc de la Communauté Financière Africaine* (African Financial Community franc).

The transformation began in the area of finances. During the conference, I gave an offering of nearly $250.00 (125,000 FCFA) to answer the call of the pastors to contribute to the organizational costs. I had never been that generous in a church before. In Cameroon, my offering rarely exceeded $1.00 (500 FCFA). I never heeded the call to the faithful to contribute to a special project. I considered that the church should be able to finance the projects it undertook without requiring an additional contribution. Besides not contributing much to the collection, I did not tithe either in the house of the Lord. In my perspective, the financial assistance I provided to my family and friends, as well as to the strangers on the street, was my tithing.

In Benin during the conference, before I was taught that I should share my resources with God, I received the following revelation: whatever we sow in the house of the Lord always bears fruit and is returned a hundredfold. I realized that in most cases, the blessings we receive in our lives are proportional to our commitment to his work, including the financial commitment. Furthermore, I finally understood that money was needed to advance the Kingdom of God, and that it was a privilege to contribute to that advancement. So I began to tithe and to give regularly at the collection, with generosity and from the goodness of my heart.[25]

Within Action Faith Church, my life underwent a revolution. The Lord planted a desire and love for prayer in my heart. So I began to pray intensely with others during the prayer evenings, as well as by myself in my room. In Cameroon, I had resisted praying. I did not see the need; I

---

[25] "'Bring all the tithes into the storehouse,
That there may be food in My house,
And try Me now in this,'
Says the Lord of hosts,
'If I will not open for you the windows of heaven
And pour out for you such blessing
That there will not be room enough to receive it.'" (Malachi 3:10)

relied on myself. And when I happened to pray occasionally, I asked God to fulfill my desires and projects. I took the decisions, and God should follow. I had not understood yet that He was the Creator, and I, the creature, He the potter, and I, the clay. It was up to Him then to shape me as He pleased, and to show me his plan for my life. So I began to pray that God would reveal to me his perfect will, and grant me the grace to obey Him in all circumstances.[26]

The transformation process affected many other aspects of my Christian life, such as attendance at meetings and continual worship of God through songs, as well as fellowship and Bible reading. In Cameroon, my Bible used to pick up dust all week, but in Cotonou, my heart was inflamed with a true passion for reading the Word. The Holy Scriptures, the preaching and my prayer taught me to devote myself entirely to God. I turned my back on this double life that I had led in Cameroon, and to the *one foot in and one foot out attitude* that had always been typical of me. I now stood firmly in the house of God Eternal.

These profound changes in my life brought me to question the real meaning of my presence in Benin. I had arrived in this country on May 16, 2009 with the goal of making money. Indeed, the director of communications firm had offered me a salary twice what I earned as a journalist in Cameroon. This was a godsend for me, because I would finally be able to save for my plan to go live in Canada. So I told Jean-Paul that I was committing to the job for two years, after which I would take off towards other horizons. However, the turn of events began to suggest that God was at work here: He had led me to Cotonou not because of the job, but to transform my spiritual life. My relationship with

---

[26] "But this is what I commanded them, saying, 'Obey My voice, and I will be your God, and you shall be My people. And walk in all the ways that I have commanded you, that it may be well with you.'" (Jeremiah 7:23)

Him was the real reason for my move to Benin. This was confirmed a few weeks later.

It was difficult to get the television networks to broadcast our productions. They were reluctant to sponsor our programs aimed at a public of high intellectual life. As a result, the firm had no income. In August, three months after my arrival in Cotonou, Jean-Paul told me he could not pay me anymore. Here I was, unemployed in a foreign country. The news did not shake me, however, because I was sure now that the job had only been a bait that God had used to get me out of my country, and teach me to walk in his ways.

CHAPTER 7

The Vision

*"And it shall come to pass afterward
That I will pour out My Spirit on all flesh;
Your sons and your daughters shall prophesy,
Your old men shall dream dreams,
Your young men shall see visions."
(Joel 2:28)*

The loss of my job had not had any negative impact on my spiritual life. On the opposite, my fervor and devotion for all things related to God increased. Jean-Paul provided my accommodation for free, but I was on my own for food. I lived off of my savings for a while, but at the end of October 2009, I was ready to file for bankruptcy. I did not have a penny on me, and my bank account was at zero balance. So, I depended entirely on God. The prayer, *Lord, give us this day our daily bread*, took on its full meaning. Every morning, I woke up not knowing how my daily bread would be provided; still, I was confident that God would take care of all my needs.[27]

---

[27] "Look at the birds of the air, for they neither sow nor reap nor gather into barns; yet your heavenly Father feeds them. Are you not of more value than they?" (Matthew 6:26)

My best friend Pascal called me sometimes. He invited me to share a meal with him and gave me money,[28] enough to buy food for two or three days. And when my well ran dry again, God called someone else to offer me food. Once in a while, I visited my pastor. Without any request on my part, he gave me a meal and before I left, he gave me money. This kindness on the part of the Lord nourished my faith so much that one day, I did what I thought I would never do.

Jean-Paul had given me money for a specific job I had done for him, enough to provide for my upkeep for at least two weeks. Instead of keeping that money, I gave it all to God as a sacrificial offering.[29] "Lord, I do not want to limit my life expectancy to two weeks," I began. "That's why I bring You this offering, so that You take care of me, not only during the two weeks for which this money would have provided for me, but also for the rest of my life." When I dropped my envelope in the collection basket that Sunday, I remembered what Jesus had said about the poor widow and her offering of two small coins: "Assuredly, I say to you that this poor widow has put in more than all those who have given to the treasury; for they all put in out of their abundance, but she out of her poverty put in all that she had, her whole livelihood."[30] I, too, had just given my whole livelihood...

The Lord honored his Word.[31] Every day, He took care of me, making sure I was given my daily bread, sometimes in one way, sometimes in another way. I could not foresee the source of the money or of the meals. The Lord's ways to provide were always unexpected, as that one day when Brigitte, the maid, found me crying.

---

28 "He who has pity on the poor lends to the Lord,
    And He will pay back what he has given." (Proverbs 19:17)
29 "Those who sow in tears
    Shall reap in joy." (Psalms 126:5)
30 Mark 12:43-44.
31 "And my God shall supply all your need according to His riches in glory by Christ Jesus." (Philippians 4:19)

The Vision

In tears, I was gazing upward, hoping that the manna for the day would fall from heaven. It was getting late, and no one had called me yet. Exhausted and hungry, I did not have the strength to go for a stroll in the hope of stumbling on a generous stranger, as had happened before. I had become skeletal to the point of making people wonder, like Jean-Paul's mother who had commented: "My son, you have to eat. When you arrived in Cotonou, you already were not very big, but now you have become scrawny." *But to eat, one needs food*, I thought. Actually, I did manage to put something in my mouth every day, but the quantity did not suffice, let alone the quality.

Brigitte found me in front of the veranda, despondent... in tears. She was aware of my sad story, and had always been generous with me. Whenever she had a chance, she snuck out a bit of food for me. That day, she did much more; she gave me money: $10.00 (5,000 FCFA). Such an amount of money was a big sacrifice for a poor housekeeper.

In Cameroon, such intense suffering would have prompted me to murmur against God, to feel abandoned, neglected, but here in Cotonou, it fed my passion for the Lord: He had become my all. In moments of doubt and uncertainty, it was enough for me to recite "Psalm 23" that Mom had once advised me to memorize:

The Lord is my shepherd; I shall not want.
He makes me to lie down in green pastures;
He leads me beside the still waters.
He restores my soul;
He leads me in the paths of righteousness
For His name's sake.
Yea, though I walk through the valley of the shadow of death,
I will fear no evil; For You are with me;
Your rod and Your staff, they comfort me.

You prepare a table before me
in the presence of my enemies;
You anoint my head with oil;
My cup runs over.
Surely goodness and mercy shall follow me
All the days of my life;
And I will dwell in the house of the Lord
Forever.

The valley of the shadow of death, through which I was walking, forced me to turn my heart completely towards God; I knew that I was lost without Him. I also understood that God molds his children through fire. He had to purify me, break me[32], so that I would die, and He, live in me. He had to prepare my heart for me to become a vessel of honor, capable of holding his project for my life.[33]

In these moments of extreme pain, God chose to reveal to me his plan for my life. Every day for a week, He spoke to me in visions. They were divine moments! I cannot really explain what I experienced, but I know that I was filled with a supernatural presence that gave me ideas and strategies. I had often heard people say, "God spoke to me." I thought it was ridiculous, actually. How could God speak to a person? But now, I myself was living the experience. I did not hear a voice, as some people claim to hear, but the special presence of the Holy Spirit left no trace of doubt about the divine nature of these revelations.

God was showing me projects that He would accomplish through me, his projects. In this demonstration, I was only

---

[32] "So He humbled you, allowed you to hunger, and fed you with manna which you did not know nor did your fathers know, that He might make you know that man shall not live by bread alone; but man lives by every word that proceeds from the mouth of the LORD." (Deuteronomy 8:3)

[33] "Therefore if anyone cleanses himself from the latter, he will be a vessel for honor, sanctified and useful for the Master, prepared for every good work." (2 Timothy 2:21)

the instrument selected for their implementation. He was showing me opportunities in the business world, and how I would benefit of them for the advancement of his Kingdom. He showed me wealth at a time when I was one of the poorest men on the planet. According to human logic, this could only be a joke.

Miserable, stuck in one of the poorest countries in the world, unable to provide for my own most basic needs, where was I to begin my conquest of the world? Where would I find the money required for the management studies that would equip me to realize the vision? I had better not ask too many questions, lest doubt settle in my heart. God had spoken: He would accomplish his word.[34] I chose to believe in God, and in his glorious plan for my life.

---

34   "God is not a man, that He should lie,
        Nor a son of man, that He should repent.
        Has He said, and will He not do?
        Or has He spoken, and will He not make it good?" (Numbers 23:19)

CHAPTER 8

Learning Through Faith

> *"Being confident of this very thing, that He who has begun a good work in you will complete it until the day of Jesus Christ." (Philippians 1:6)*

The news made me burst with joy: the University of Nice Sophia Antipolis had accepted my application for the Master of Business Administration program. This open door to a quality education was giving the projects of the Lord a real beginning. The opportunity to acquire the managerial knowledge I needed to support the entrepreneurial vision the Lord had shown me was being offered to me. However, in my joy, I realized that I was going a little too fast: the admission was only the first step towards this quality education. I had yet to find the necessary funding.

The two-year program cost over $8,000.00, more than $4,000.00 a year. Registration fees amounted to a little over $600.00, for a grand total of about $8,600.00.[35] The program was completely offered on-line, but the students were required to be present at the University of Nice at the end of each year for the exams. Adding the travel expenses for two trips to Nice in the south of France, the total budget of

---

35   4,200,000.00 FCFA.

this master's program amounted to a little over $12,000.00,[36] an astronomical sum for a young man who was barely surviving, not a penny to his name.

I had taken steps to follow this master's course about two months after my arrival in Cotonou. I still had money then. My salary allowed me to fund these studies in installments over two years. I had no idea that I would find myself unemployed overnight... By the beginning of October 2009, my financial situation had bottomed out. What good was it to be admitted to the master's program if I had no money to fund it? I had to make a choice: throw in the towel and forget about it, or be bold and continue to believe.

I chose to be bold. I was going to fight, at least to collect the $600.00 for the admission to the program; I would then be guaranteed my place. God would help me later to find the $8,000.00 to pay for the whole program. My hopes to make it through were high, since the university offered the option of spreading the payments over the duration of the program, on the only condition that one have a bank account in France. I contacted my friend Nicole, with whom I had attended the audition at the radio station seven years earlier. She lived in Paris.

Nicole agreed to open a bank account on my behalf, from which the university would withdraw $825.00[37] every other month. So I would have to make regular transfers into that bank account. Nicole should not pay a penny for my studies, of course. She simply eased my participation in the financing plan offered by the university. Nevertheless, she was my guarantor; she would have to face the law if ever I defaulted on my payments. She was, therefore, taking a huge risk for me, in the name of our friendship.

The bimonthly payments to the university were to begin in February 2010. I had some time left; hope was good. In

---
36   About 6 million FCFA.
37   400,000.00 FCFA.

four months, God could turn my situation around and give me a job that would allow me to meet my commitments, but right now, I had to find the $600.00 registration fees. Nicole was waiting for that money to open a bank account, and start the automatic debiting procedure for the Institute of Business Administration of the University of Nice.

The deadline for the payment of the registration fees was October 30, 2009. So I had about three weeks to find $600.00. I prayed God to give me that money, convinced that this plan of studies for me was his. Had He not given me himself a vision that required that I study? Surely, God would not contradict Himself; He would move someone's heart to lend me the $600.00 I needed. I called several family members and friends to inform them of the situation, but no one could help me. I became depressed!

For the first time in my life, I experienced insomnia. Plagued with worries, I could not sleep for seven nights. My thoughts kept returning to the money that I had to find at all costs. With each passing day, my hopes weakened. I worried, and I panicked: would I miss such a great opportunity? My life had become a wreck; this master's program was a lifesaver. If I failed to grab it, I would sink into the depths of the abyss. Discouraged, I had exhausted all possibilities of solving this problem with my own strength. At that point, God Eternal walked on stage.

One week before the deadline, I had a discussion with Nicole. She wondered why I still had not sent her the $600.00. I mumbled poor excuses, and said that the money would be available shortly. She realized that I had financial difficulties. Without my asking, she offered to lend me the money. I remained speechless at this miracle that God was performing. I reassured Nicole that the money would be repaid in a few weeks, as she wanted, even though I had no idea where it would come from. God had just put in Nicole's heart the desire to lend me money; that same God would help

Learning Through Faith

me repay it, despite a tight deadline. The Lord had just given me the unexpected opportunity to register at the University of Nice; of course, He would not stop halfway. For sure, He would allow me to repay Nicole and later pay $825.00 bimonthly to the university. When the Lord sets his hand at a task, He sees it through.[38]

Nicole made sure that all the formalities for my registration were met. The university sent her the administrative file by mail on Monday, October 26, 2009. She received it Wednesday, October 28th, filled the forms and returned them. Friday, October 30th, the university took delivery of the signed documents, and finalized my registration for the Master in Business Administration. So I was registered in the program at the very last minute, the last day of registrations. I understood that God is never late: He comes at the right time.

The time came to pay my debt to Nicole. She urgently needed the money for her own academic registration. I turned to the One who had begun this whole thing. God had touched Nicole's heart; He had inspired her to lend me the money, without any request on my part. So it was up to Him to assume responsibility. I relied on Him for a new job, or simply for a gift from an unknown person, so that I could be free of my debt. I asked Nicole to give me an extension.

After a while, Nicole insisted. I was still unable to pay my debt, and the deadline for her registration was approaching. I felt bad, ashamed and powerless in this situation. Nicole had placed all her trust in me, and I was letting her down. The friendship that we had built over ten years was about to collapse overnight. To my physical breakdown was added an extreme moral suffering. I felt guilty for abusing the trust of a friend. I had not told her that I had lost my job when she had offered to lend me the money, lest she should reconsider.

---

[38] "...being confident of this very thing, that He who has begun a good work in you will complete it until the day of Jesus Christ." (Philippians 1:6)

That was my fault. My conviction of being able to repay her the $600.00 had been based on God, on his ability to meet all my needs. Now I felt that God was not paying me any attention anymore. Why had He allowed me to receive this money if He knew beforehand that He would not help me repay it? Why had He supported my university registration if He knew that Nicole would miss hers on account of mine? Could God help me at the expense of someone else?

Tired of all those questions, I focused on the future. I did not want to stay in Cotonou, a city unable to provide me with a job. I felt inside the desire, the need to go live in Abidjan, the capital of Ivory Coast. At least, I would have a chance to find work over there. The city was flourishing economically; I had often admired it for that, already when I was still living in Cameroon. But was it God's will? To find out, I asked God to finance the trip.

Miracle! A few days later, in December 2009, my former boss told me about a work project in Dakar, Senegal. His firm had been selected to manage communications at an international conference in Dakar. Jean-Paul needed my services as a freelance reporter. This five-day stay in Dakar provided the money for my trip to Abidjan.

The money did not solve everything. I still had to find a place to stay in the Ivorian capital. I remembered Raymond, a friend I had met at an international conference only two days after my arrival in Cotonou. He was working in a financial institution in Abidjan. From the very first moments of our meeting, we hit it off well. At that time, I was dreaming of going to Canada. My plan was to work in Cotonou for two years, and then fly off to Montreal in Quebec. I did not know that the Lord had already made plans for my future. He had led me to Raymond in the first hours of my presence in Benin, because his plan was to take me to Abidjan. Consequently, young Daniel's prophecy took on all its meaning for me. "Africa, Africa..." I realized that my African adventures with God would not be limited to Cotonou... No surprise then that Raymond agreed to welcome me in his home in Abidjan.

Before leaving, I shared my testimony in church during worship. I talked about the spiritual transformation that the Lord had brought about in my life. I had become a more mature Christian, seasoned to spiritual warfare. I had acquired this spiritual maturity at the cost of great suffering: my bony and emaciated face provided clear evidence, but behind this physical fragility, a strong spirit was hiding. In faith, I had become a giant!

Conference in Dakar, Senegal, December 2009.

Chapter 9
Persevering Through Hardships

"And not only that, but we also glory in tribulations, knowing that tribulation produces perseverance; and perseverance, character, and character, hope." (Romans 5:3-4)

When I trod the Ivorian soil on the morning of January 7, 2010, the beauty of the landscape struck me; I could have thought I was back in Cameroon. I had just arrived in Noé, the first city in Ivory Coast, on the border with Ghana. It had been a long trip. The bus had left Cotonou the day before, at around noon, and had crossed Togo and Ghana completely. Since the passengers had to get off the bus for customs, I took the opportunity to stretch my legs. I was in Ivory Coast!

A few hours later, I arrived in Abidjan. Raymond's house was located in the upscale neighborhood of the Riviera. Besides the beautiful villa, the property had a guesthouse that allowed me some privacy, away from the hubbub of the children. I learned that Raymond had moved into this house only two months earlier. He had left his small apartment for a bigger house to accommodate his wife and three children, who had arrived from another country. However, I had good reason to believe that an invisible hand had guided his choice for this specific place in anticipation of my arrival.

Francis, Raymond's work colleague, lived only a stone's throw away. I had made the acquaintance of Francis in Cotonou at the same conference where I had met Raymond. On the evening of the first day of the conference, Jean-Paul had introduced me to Francis. Right away, he had said that he recognized me from somewhere, but could not remember exactly from where. I told him that I had been a television reporter. He recalled then that he had seen me on television in Abidjan.

So seven months later, I had landed in Abidjan, in the hands of two people whom I had met at the beginning of what I now call my West African pilgrimage. With Raymond, I had room and board, but the house was not connected to the Internet, which I needed for my master's program on-line. Francis had an Internet connection in his house. He gave me carte blanche to use it as needed. The roles had then been assigned: God had it all planned.

Without any money at all, I depended entirely on these two friends. The money from the project in Dakar had served for the trip to Abidjan. So I was flat broke again. I could not ask Raymond for money; he graciously housed me and fed me for free. I could not ask Francis either; he gave me access to the on-line training platform. I was left on my own. Had I not come to Abidjan to search for a job?

I checked my address book, and contacted a few people I had met at the international conferences I had attended. They held important positions in large companies in Abidjan. I had high hopes that I'd be recommended by one of them, but after a few weeks, I became disillusioned. One of the deepest disappointments related to a possible position in a radio station. A friend put me in touch with a journalist working in that station. She was looking for a collaborator for her radio program. So I had arrived at the right time for this dream job. But the dream was cut short! The journalist changed her mind overnight: she did not need any assistance.

Disappointed, I continued my job search by consulting the professional networks on the Internet. That's how I found the director of a consulting firm. He was interested in my profile, but could not see me until April 2010 because he was traveling in the United States. I did not give much weight to this correspondence; I needed a job right now, not in three months. I doubled my efforts in vain. I became completely depressed.

I had stopped praying; I was not reading the Bible anymore. My strength was depleted, as my desire. It really felt like fate was dogging me.[39] How could anyone live like this? Since I had lost my father at ten years old twenty years earlier, all I had known was suffering. Was I born to suffer? No, I would not give up. God's visions in Cotonou had revealed a bright future for me, but I did not understand his method: was it compulsory to walk through pain to become the person He had in mind?

I had been a Christian for ten years now, ever since the events of 1997 in the small town of Mfou, south of Yaoundé. My Christian life had been a bumpy ride between compromise and repentance. In Cameroon, I had been neither hot nor cold for the Lord. My Christian life had been more of a routine. I had reserved myself the right to put God in the closet whenever it suited me. After living a moribund Christian life for more than ten years, I remained a spiritual dwarf. God decided to wake me from my coma, and to make me grow.

In my fertile imagination, I read my situation as follow: I was seventeen years old when God saved me. He had

---

[39] "Why are you cast down, O my soul?
And why are you disquieted within me?
Hope in God;
For I shall yet praise Him,
The help of my countenance and my God." (Psalms 42:11)

given me time to grow throughout the years, so that I would become spiritually mature and be able to lead the mission He had planned for me in this world. But ten years after my conversion, I was still content with spiritual milk, refusing to grow up. God decided to react. He called a meeting in heaven to debate about my fate: let me continue in my casual way to the risk of wasting my potential and not meeting expectations, or resort to the hard way and bring me back on the right path? The verdict was delivered: the hard way! I was to leave for a period of intense training in Cotonou and Abidjan, where God would enroll me in his school of suffering and perseverance, so that I would assimilate in a few months what I had not learned in ten years of Christian life. That was the meaning of my journey impressed with a seal of pain. "Africa, Africa…," my walk through the desert.

Had young Daniel revealed what lay behind this prophecy, "Africa, Africa…", spoken to me while I was in Cameroon, I probably would have resisted the call, preferring to remain in my desperate state. Besides, did he know the exact meaning of these words? Had God been content with giving him the words without their meaning? Anyway, it was too late to turn back; I was already enrolled in that particular school of God, reserved for the people chosen to accomplish great things. This school builds character, brings one closer to God, and leads to refocus life on the essential, namely give God complete freedom as He accomplishes the plan He has for us.

Revived by this revelation, I decided to focus my attention on the purpose of the test, and not on the test itself. It was intended to make me grow spiritually, and to strip me of anything that was an obstacle on my glorious path in Jesus Christ. Surely there was a reward at the end of this suffering, so I had to stand firm to wear the crown reserved for those

A Letter to God

who persevere to the end.[40] After the crossing of the desert comes the Promised Land, flowing with milk and honey. I decided not to complain against God, lest my days in the desert be lengthened, as had been the case for the children of Israel. I suffered too much to take such a risk.

I found my way back to church. Sunday mornings, I attended a worship service in a church nearby. During the week, I visited another Christian community that met in a private home and offered biblical teachings. I discovered this community during a stroll in my neighborhood. I heard a stranger's telephone ring. The ringtone was a Christian song: rather surprising! Curious, I approached the young man who assured me that he was a Christian and pointed to a beautiful villa, right in front of us, where a small group of Christians met on Tuesday and Thursday evenings. Deep within me, I knew that this meeting was not a product of chance…

---

40   "And not only that, but we also glory in tribulations, knowing that tribulation produces perseverance; and perseverance, character; and character, hope." (Romans 5:3-4)

Chapter 10

Against All Hope

*"But those who wait on the LORD
Shall renew their strength;
They shall mount up with wings like eagles,
They shall run and not be weary,
They shall walk and not faint."
(Isaiah 40:31)*

The ultimatum had been delivered: I had two days to leave the house. That evening, Raymond had been firm, and his decision was final. I had been living at his place for two months, and I still had not found a job, allowing me to stand on my own feet. From the beginning, we had agreed that I would not stay at his place more than two months. So he was totally within his rights, and I could not blame him. How could I be angry with the person who had given me free room and board so graciously for two months?[41] He had been patient up to that evening, when his voice had gone up a notch.

---

41   "If you extend your soul to the hungry
And satisfy the afflicted soul,
Then your light shall dawn in the darkness,
And your darkness shall be as the noonday." (Isaiah 58:10)

Two weeks earlier, Raymond had suggested that I start thinking about my next step. His words had made me panic. I had nowhere to go in this foreign country. Moreover, I was still unemployed, unable to take care of myself. I mentioned the situation to one of the pastors at my church. I was hoping that he would let me sleep in the church a few days, just long enough to find work and fly with my own wings. The pastor gave me this answer, which surprised me as much as it disappointed me: "We no longer accept that brothers sleep in the church. Only one person sleeps in the church, the guardian who watches it. It's a pity you have only been coming to church for a few weeks; in addition, you come from a foreign country. If I knew you better, I could recommend you to a few brothers who could accommodate you. But I cannot take that risk…"

The service was over: I could not count on the help of my church. When I was still in Cameroon, I would have left the church because of such words by a pastor. But here in Abidjan, God had made me a spiritual man. I was here to serve Him, and to listen to his will; I had learned that some things He allows for his glory, present or future. If I left a church every time its pastor did not show any charity, never would I belong to a church.

I realized that it was easier for me to abandon myself entirely in the hands of God, after my own resources had failed. In this case, I had placed my hopes in a man of God, but I was disappointed. Henceforth, I would trust in God alone.[42] So when Raymond delivered the ultimatum that evening in February 2010, I remained impervious, confident that the Lord was in control.

Before sleeping that night, I made this prayer to God: "Lord, Your Word says that no test is above our strength. If

---

42   "Commit your way to the LORD,
     Trust also in Him,
     And He shall bring it to pass." (Psalms 37:5)

You believe that I have the strength required to undergo this test, then I accept it as a challenge, confident You are with me. If, on the opposite, You judge that this test is beyond my strength, then I pray that You take it away."

I slept peacefully that night. I had let go of a heavy burden. The case belonged to God. He would solve it his way: or I was kicked out of the house, in which case God was responsible to fortify me, feed me and protect me[43], while I remained without a home; or He would find a solution to my housing problem. The burden was no longer mine. I had taken a giant step in faith. My trust in God was complete; I knew He would find a solution to my problem.

The next day, Raymond sent me an email. He had changed his mind. He had thought about it all night: I could stay with him until I found a job. He did not offer me an extension of one or two months only, but he gave me a blank check to remain in the house until my situation allowed me to fly with my own wings. I discovered how good God is, and how trustworthy is his Word. God had brought about a change of heart in Raymond; my problem was solved.

In April 2010, Catherine, a friend from Cotonou, came to Abidjan for a work assignment. I borrowed money from Francis's housekeeper to visit Catherine at her hotel. Since she knew my situation, I expected that she would give me a little bit of money at the end of our exchange, if only the amount borrowed from the housekeeper. I was not disappointed; on the contrary, her generosity exceeded all my expectations. She gave me a $20.00 bill (10,000 FCFA). I thought she had given me $5.00; since the conference in Dakar, four months earlier, I had not seen such a big bill.

I had struck gold: four months without any need of money. The Lord had contrived everything: Raymond was providing me free room and board; Francis let me use the

---

[43] "He who dwells in the secret place of the Most High
Shall abide under the shadow of the Almighty." (Psalms 91:1)

Internet without a fee; the church and the home Christian community were only a few steps away... a perfect spiritual ecosystem where money had become obsolete. God was teaching me to rely on Him, and not on money.

I came back home late that night. Catherine had insisted that I share dinner with her and a few of her friends from Abidjan. Back at the villa, I found the household already asleep. I walked in the neighborhood through the night, looking for a place to sleep. Finally, a night watchman gave me his wooden bench that served as his berth: my first night under the stars...

As was to be expected, I woke up the next day completely stiff. This unplanned physical pain added to my mental anguish. It was not easy to take the humiliation I was a subject of at the house. Contempt did not come from Raymond, who showed me respect—to a certain point—but from the maid. How could a maid despise a former great reporter like me? I'll admit that she did not know me when I was a public figure, but was that a reason to patronize me?

If a maid could think more highly of herself than of me, I must have been very pitiful... At least she was working to earn her daily bread; I was totally dependent on Raymond's goodwill to support me. If anything, the maid was right. This showed me how low I had fallen, to what point God had belittled me. He had done it to teach me to live in humility, even humiliation. I was discovering a completely new aspect of this school I was enrolled in: the school of glory, a glory that digs its roots in humility.[44] So I put away my pride of former great journalist in the drawer of my memories. The condescending attitude of the housekeeper did not affect me anymore, nor did the smiles of pity I got from people around

---

44   "The fear of the Lord is the instruction of wisdom,
And before honor is humility." (Proverbs 15:33)

me. I had decided not to measure my worth according to the eyes of men, but of God.[45]

Often people were critical of my studies. When I told them that I was studying for a master's in business administration at the University of Nice, they smirked, clearly letting me see that according to them, I was ready to cling to anything out of despair, even to that which was evidently not worth the trouble. It is true that from a logical point of view, I should have abandoned these studies. First, I did not have the means to pay for the program... I had not been able to meet the February and April bank withdrawal deadlines. I was aware that this default caused trouble for Nicole. Poor her! I still had not repaid the $600.00 I owed her. In addition, I did not have any money to fund my trip to Nice for the exams in July... but that was needed only if my entry visa to France was granted.

Far from letting this cruel situation get me down, I chose to rely on God. I would not lower God Eternal to the level of human logic: I would live my faith... Since the online platform training was still available, despite the missed payments, I continued to work at my classes and to submit my assignments as if all was in order. This was an extraordinary act of faith.[46] Despite the winds of doubt and uncertainty around me, I kept my eyes fixed on the God who commands the winds and the storms. No matter what appeared in my line of vision, I stayed focused on the vision that the Lord had shown me in Cotonou. He would certainly clear a path for me.

---

[45] "...For the Lord does not see as man sees; for man looks at the outward appearance, but the Lord looks at the heart." (1 Samuel 16:7)
[46] "...all things are possible to him who believes." (Mark 9:23)

CHAPTER 11

Faith in Action

"What does it profit, my brethren, if someone says he has faith but does not have works?"
(James 2:14)

Pastor Roger's suggestion during the Bible study that Thursday night left us all speechless: write a letter to God! "How can one write a letter to God?" exclaimed the members of the assembly, incredulous. "Why write a letter when a simple oral prayer suffices for God to hear us? Besides, how can one send a letter to a Divine Being?" Obviously, we could not count on the local Post Office to deliver our mail to heaven; they already had their hands full with the postal services on earth.

These remarks, tinged with derision, did not shake the serenity of the pastor, who was convinced that God had inspired him to present his suggestion. In our letter, we were to relate our problems to God, and ask Him to solve them. Many did not take the exercise seriously. As for me, I was immersed in such destitution that any idea likely to get me out of my misery was welcomed. Of course, like everyone else, the idea of writing a letter to God seemed to me devoid of common sense, but after a moment's reflection, I surrendered: this illogical act was the kind God loves to use to manifest his glory. After all, did not the nature of my problems require a supernatural intervention of God?

The next day, sitting on my mattress on the floor, I decided to write my letter to God. I understood that only an exceptional faith could remove the mountain of obstacles that stood before me.[47] I prayed to the Holy Spirit to give me the inspiration to write this letter, according to the will of God. I wrote it as a cover letter. I dedicated to it the same care and determination I would have to convince an employer to hire me. I introduced myself to God as his legitimate child, reminding Him of his promises. I asked Him what I thought corresponded to the vision He had revealed to me in Cotonou.

Abidjan, April 20, 2010
ONGOLO Antoine Désiré
Legitimate child of God (John 1:12)
Tel. : +2 256 503 1039
E-mail :antonydesy@yahoo.fr

My Lord and Savior JESUS CHRIST

RE *: John 16:24 "Until now you have asked nothing in My name. Ask, and you will receive, that your joy may be full."*

Dear My Lord and Savior Jesus Christ,

I hereby humbly come to submit my prayer requests to You. You said in your Word: "Come to Me all you who are weary and burdened, and I will give you rest." **God Eternal**, *I come seeking rest in You, knowing that only You are able to meet my needs.*

Based on your Word, that says in the sixth verse of the fourth chapter of Philippians: "Be anxious for nothing, but in everything by prayer and supplication, with thanksgiving, let your requests be made known to God;

---

[47] "For assuredly, I say to you, whoever says to this mountain, 'Be removed and be cast into the sea,' and does not doubt in his heart, but believes that those things he says will be done, he will have whatever he says." (Mark 11:23)

and the peace of God, which surpasses all understanding, will guard your hearts and minds through Christ Jesus," I am honored to inform You of my major needs:
1. *Find a job in the very short term (days and weeks);*
2. *Be included among the young African leaders who will attend the seminar in Johannesburg, South Africa in late May 2010;*
3. *Find the money for the plane ticket, accommodation, food and the visa to go to Nice, France in late June for the master's exams;*
4. *In the medium term (weeks and months), find a job or an internship at the international level, and provide for travel, accommodation and food;*
5. *Find $4,000.00 before July 5, 2010 to pay for the first year of the master's program;*
6. *Be in perfect physical and mental health, and benefit of God's permanent protection for myself and for my family;*
7. *By the end of this year, find a beautiful and virtuous woman who will be my wife;*
8. *Win the U.S. lottery for the* **green card** *this year.*

My Lord and Savior Jesus Christ,

You said: "Call upon Me in the day of trouble; I will deliver you, and you shall glorify Me."48 I pray that You grant all my prayer requests, according to Your own schedule. **God Eternal**, *I entrust my fate into Your hands, I put my full trust in You and I know that You will take action, because* **Scriptures** *do not lie. In addition, I have* **faith**. *Yet, You say in verse twenty-four of the eleventh chapter in Mark: "Therefore I say to you, whatever things you ask when you pray, believe that you receive them, and you will have them."*

Lord, I believe that I have already received all that I have just asked You. I thank You very much for everything You already have done in my life, for all that You do every day and for all that You will do. In the name of **JESUS CHRIST**. *Amen.*

---

48 Psalms 50:15

Faith in Action

Seeing my letter, Pastor Roger could not hide his surprise. Obviously, he had not expected such an endeavor on my part. I had composed a formal spiritual cover letter... It was serious! The other members of the congregation, who had dared to perform the exercise, had been content with a few words scribbled on a piece of paper.

According to the pastor, my queries to the Lord were completely unrealistic... The purpose had not been to daydream! I had to keep my feet on the ground, be realistic... I was a young man, poor and unemployed, who lived at the expense of someone else. A logical request to the Lord would have been to ask Him to find me a job so that I could be independent, and eventually establish myself in Abidjan.

Instead, I asked thousands of dollars (millions of FCFA) to the Lord; I asked Him for an international internship; I asked Him to grant me a visa for my studies in France; I asked Him to live in the United States soon... In short, I asked the impossible. I was completely idealistic about my situation in Abidjan.

Despite the pastor's critique, I did not move an inch. Is faith not the substance of things hoped for, the evidence of things not seen?[49] I had faith that my requests would be carried out; then, I should not show the slightest doubt. Besides, my requests were not fantasies to me, because I believed in the glorious future that the Lord had revealed in the visions of Cotonou. The pastor was impressed by my great faith... We prayed together; my letter remained in the hands of God.

---

[49] Hebrews 11:1

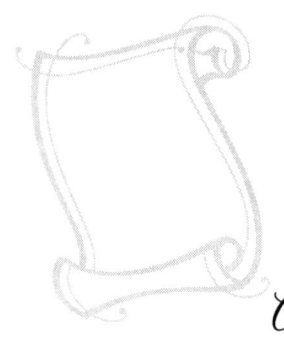

CHAPTER 12

At the Crossroads

*"Thus says the LORD: Stand in the ways and see,
And ask for the old paths, where the good way is,
And walk in it..."*
(Jeremiah 6:16)

The validity of my visa on Ivorian soil was expiring soon. I needed $80.00 (40,000 FCFA) to renew it. One of my younger sisters in Cameroon sent me half of that amount. I had to find $40.00 (20,000 FCFA). I was unemployed; the problem seemed unsolvable. Only God could help me. I implored Him to take care of this financial need so that I'd retain my legal status in Ivory Coast. An illegal status could jeopardize my chances of getting a visa for France later. I left this burden at the feet of the Lord, just as I had done when Raymond had asked me to leave. I forgot about it, living as if the problem had already been solved.

I was still looking for a job; I remembered the director of the consulting firm I had contacted through a professional network three months earlier. He had promised to return to Abidjan in April, and had been ready to grant me an interview. I called him, and we set an appointment.

Mr. Konan received me in his impressive home, which also served as headquarters for his consulting firm. He was looking for someone to manage the daily business of his office. I had the right profile.

At the end of the interview, Mr. Konan offered to cover the taxi fare. I was very surprised by his proposal; I never imagined that an employer could give money to a job applicant on the day of the interview. The fare from the firm to my home amounted to $0.60 (300 FCFA). I thought he'd give me a few dollars, ten at the most (5,000 FCFA). Mr. Konan first pulled a $20.00 bill (10,000 FCFA) from his wallet, then a second... He gave me $40.00, the exact sum I needed to renew my visa... on the day before it expired.

I held back my tears in front of him. Once outside though, I let go. The abundant flow of my tears was only equaled by the joy and gratitude I felt for my God. Even in my wildest dreams, I had never imagined that the Lord could support me this way: an employer who gives money to a job applicant on the day of the interview! More than ever, I knew that nothing is impossible to God: He blesses us as He wishes, at times using methods contrary to human logic. That day, my faith grew by a notch.

A few days later, Mr. Konan hired me. For the first time since I had lost my job in Benin in August of the previous year, I had found my way back to work. The Lord had just granted the first request of my letter.

I received a salary at regular intervals for my office work. These were not large amounts, but it was enough to give me a bit of dignity and respectability. I could now provide for my basic needs. However, my situation was precarious because my income still did not allow me to afford a home. My hopes then turned to another direction: South Africa.

A seminar for young African leaders was to be held in South Africa in May 2010. I had applied to take part in this meeting. The organizers ensured transport and accommodation. I longed to be chosen, hoping to live in the richest country in Africa, even settle down there... The seminar was to last a week, and then the participants return to their respective countries. I secretly harbored the desire not to return to Abidjan. I was planning to stay with one of my best friends, who had been living in Johannesburg for two years already. I trusted that he would help me legalize my situation in South Africa.

My heart was torn between the lure of this clandestine adventure in South Africa and God's promises regarding my future in Europe. Well, I was still confident that God would take me to France for my studies, but at the same time I was ready to seize the first opportunity to get out of Abidjan. Were the two paths necessarily incompatible? God could always take me to France from Johannesburg... but my situation in South Africa would have to be legal. Deep down, I knew that I had to wait patiently for God to lead me to France from Abidjan;[50] but I also knew that if I were to be chosen to attend the seminar, I would not resist the temptation to stay in South Africa illegally. I did not want to face this choice; I relied on God to deliver me from the temptation...

---

50   "The testing of your faith produces patience." (James 1:3)

CHAPTER 13

The Valley of the Shadow of Death

"Yea, though I walk through the valley of the shadow of death, I will fear no evil; For You are with me; Your rod and Your staff, they comfort me." (Psalms 23:4)

The time had come to put my faith to the test.[51] If I really believed that God would take me to France, I had to start the paperwork for the visa. Each step in the creation of the file required expenses that would greatly affect my monthly budget. It was a risky endeavor, because a denial would result in a useless financial loss. Even if the visa was granted to me, I still did not have the money for the trip and the studies. My salary was not sufficient for me to pay for the plane ticket, much less the $8,000.00 for the master's program. Did it make any sense then to start the application process for the visa? By beginning the process, I would show that my faith was strong enough to believe that God would not only give me the visa, but also defray the expenses for transport, university and accommodation during my stay in France.

---

51   "For as the body without the spirit is dead, so faith without works is dead also." (James 2:26)

Despite my failure to meet the bimonthly payments, the university had informed me that my status as a registered student authorized me to take the exams. However, I still had the obligation to pay for the program if I wanted to be enrolled in the second year, and therefore hope to get my master's degree. Nevertheless, it was good news! My immediate challenge consisted in getting the visa and the plane ticket. I could worry later about paying for the university.

I began to gather the documents needed for my visa file. I was planning to request a short-stay visa that would allow me to take the exams in Nice, and then come back to Abidjan. I had all my official registration documents from the University of Nice and the notification to attend the exams. In addition, I obtained a hotel room confirmation in Nice for the exams session. My file was complete; I was confident that I would get a short-stay visa for France.

Yet, God chose to disturb my confidence. Instead of a short-stay visa, He asked me to apply for a long-stay student visa of one year. I had learned to recognize this inner voice, the voice of the Holy Spirit, who used to give me instructions and advice. I was convinced that God was asking me to make this change. In a sense, I was delighted because I wanted to live in France, but in another sense, it weakened my case.

I was enrolled at the University of Nice in the on-line program via the Internet. As such, it was difficult to qualify for a long-stay student visa because I did not need to reside in France to complete the program I was enrolled in. As much as the short-stay visa for the exams was a logical choice, the request for a long-stay student visa was precarious and risky. By opting for such a visa, my case was weakened, almost inviting a denial by the French consulate. Was it a risk worth taking?

I chose to risk it. After all, God was asking me to apply for a long-stay visa. He is able to do all things, even those that seem impossible. I was aware that my application for a long-stay visa did not hold water, but God could make the French authorities find logic in it. If at all possible, God had chosen the means to take me to Europe. I remembered the second part of young Daniel's prophecy: " Europe, Europe." He had not only mentioned Africa. He had said: "Africa, Africa, ...Europe, Europe." If the part about Africa had come true, why would not the part about Europe also come true? Daniel's prophecy revived my hope, and I took the step in faith on the path to a long-stay student visa.

The first step on this path was to gather a parallel file for Campus France. That institution is responsible for reviewing and approving all study projects in France. Once approved, the file is sent to the Consulate of France, who takes the final decision. So I submitted my application to Campus France, and an interview was scheduled.

My morale was low after the interview; I doubted that my application would fall in a good ear. The agent at Campus France had hammered at the absurdity of my visa application. She could not understand that I'd want to do my second year of studies in France, when I was enrolled in an on-line program. When I told her that I intended to do an internship in a French company for my dissertation at the end of the program, she retorted that several French companies were present in Abidjan. In fact, I had to agree with her, but I still had the right to hope for an internship in France. I had asked God in my letter, and I believed that He would grant it to me.

The lady at Campus France remained skeptical: in her opinion, I would hit a wall if I persisted in asking a long-stay student visa. Considering my file, she did not think it wise to pursue that option. So she advised me to apply for a short-stay visa: "You have all the chances of getting a short-stay visa that will allow you to pass your exams in Nice, and then come back to Abidjan." Her word against the Lord's. Obviously, this employee did not understand that we were not on the same level, she and I; I was coming from a vision of faith that doesn't require one to walk by sight, but in the Spirit.[52] I told her that I did not intend to change my stance. My long-stay student application was therefore sent to the Consulate of France at my own risk.

When I arrived at the consulate on Monday, June 28, 2010, my arguments were ready, but I did not know that an angel of God Eternal had preceded me to smooth the way... Indeed, the consular agent did not offer any negative comment about my file. On the opposite, she made this startling statement: "Normally, it takes two weeks to process a student visa, because the answer must come from Paris, but since your master's exams begin on July 5, I will tag your file as urgent so that you get the long-stay visa within one week." She asked me to come back to the consulate the following Friday to pick up my visa. What a joy!

Back in our neighborhood, I stood in the street looking at the villa for a long while, as if to say goodbye to the house that had sheltered me for seven months. This was going to be my last week in it before flying off to France. Coincidence! This was also Raymond and his family's last week in that house. Indeed, he had begun building his own house shortly before my arrival in Abidjan. The new house was now built; it was time for him to leave this villa in the Riviera. The coincidence of these events was really surprising.

Raymond was getting ready to move out of the house exactly when I did not need it anymore; I was leaving Ivory Coast. This confirmed to me that God had led him to rent this villa, only a stone's throw from Francis's house, in order to meet my housing and my study needs during my stay in Abidjan. Thus, Raymond really could not have thrown me out of the house, as he had thought of doing in February, because God controlled his mind without him ever realizing it.

---

[52] "...The just shall live by faith." (Romans 1:27)

On Friday, July 2nd, we emptied the premises. I temporarily entrusted my personal belongings with Pastor Roger, who lived next door, and then I went to the Consulate of France to pick up my visa... Surprise! Paris had not yet responded to my request. I had to return to the consulate on Monday, July 5th, the day my exams began in Nice. It was a hard blow! For a moment, I thought I'd go crazy. Definitely, I did not understand God's methods. How could He feed my hope, and lead me to fail at the same time? The lady at Campus France had been right: I should have asked for a short-stay visa.

Everybody around me blamed me for my choice of a long-stay visa. For them, as for me, this delay until Monday was the harbinger of a likely denial of the student visa. In addition, it was now clear that I would miss the final exams of the first year; the master's program was over for me. What a mess! And to think that I had studied hard, ignored the mocking, trusted that God would reward my faith.

This last event seriously shook my faith. I did not know what to think anymore. It had seemed to me that God had inspired me to request a long-stay visa. Had I not heard well? Had I mistaken my own thoughts for those of the Lord? And if that were the case, why had He let me get lost in this error? I was puzzled.[53]

To search for respite from this psychological pressure, I decided to watch a football game on television. That July 2 evening, in the quarterfinals of the World Cup, Ghana played against Uruguay. An entire continent was riveted on this African team, on which all hope now rested. Personally, I thought that a victory for Ghana would not only honor me

---

[53] "Fear not, for I am with you;
Be not dismayed, for I am your God.
I will strengthen you,
Yes, I will help you,
I will uphold you with
My righteous right hand." (Isaiah 41:10)

A Letter to God

as an African, but also rekindle the flame of hope within. I needed to know that I could still meet the many challenges that came my way... Unfortunately, the football game destroyed what little hope I had left. Ghana's *unfair* defeat on the day I was hoping to get my visa might be confirmation that my fate was sealed.

My troubles were not over... That night, I slept on a mat on the floor, because all other beds in Pastor Roger's house were occupied. He had not appreciated the impromptu manner with which I had dropped my belongings at his home. The next day, my friend Christian offered to help me. It was not the first time that God placed him on my path. A few days earlier, I had graciously given him much of my clothes and a pair of shoes in anticipation of my departure for France. He wanted to return the favor by inviting me to his place. With two other homeless men, he temporarily occupied an abandoned house, unfinished and unsanitary. I spent the night from Saturday to Sunday in that strange house without a full roof... at the mercy of thieves.

On Sunday evening, I was making my way back to that prison cell when, suddenly, one of the housemates raised objections to my entrance. According to him, Christian had violated the rules by admitting a fourth homeless man without the consent of the other housemates. Disappointed and humiliated, I had become homeless in the middle of the night. Christian did not abandon me in this hardship; we went in search of a roof together. After walking around in the night for a while, Christian had the idea to knock on the door of his church; someone was there 24/7. That's where we found our shelter... in the house of the Lord![54] I walked towards the altar and dropped my mat next to the pulpit, where the pastor stands for the sermon.

---

54   "God is our refuge and strength,
     A very present help in trouble." (Psalms 46:1)

Monday morning, Christian and I came across the roommate who had refused to let me sleep in the abandoned house. I was surprised to see him wearing the clothes and shoes that I had given to Christian. Apparently, the three roommates shared their clothes. The young man would not look at me in the eyes; he knew where his clothes came from. His malice was out in the open: he had had the audacity to wear the clothes of a person he had left homeless in the night; he had dared to wear my clothes, after refusing to let me sleep in the abandoned house where he himself stayed by charity. *If the owner decided to resume the construction of the house, what would come of this young man? Where would he go?* I kept these questions to myself, leaving the culprit to face his own conscience.[55]

As if my mind had been renewed, I perceived these sufferings of the past few days as the last contractions of childbirth.[56] In church, I had been taught that adversity often increases when the moment of glory is near: the devil uses this strategy to extinguish our faith at the doorstep of the Promised Land. I pulled myself together[57], and repented for having doubted God and his ability to pull me out of my troubles. Surely, God Eternal was still able to give me a student visa, and to bring my studies to completion. Even if I missed the final exams of the first year, God Eternal could still save my master. Nothing is impossible to Him.

---

55   "Hatred stirs up strife,
        But love covers all sins." (Proverbs 10:12)
56   "Many are the afflictions of the righteous,
        But the LORD delivers him out of them all." (Psalms 34:19)
57   "I can do all things through Christ who strengthens me." (Philippians 4:13)

CHAPTER 14

God is Faithful

"Let us hold fast the confession of our hope without wavering, For He who promised is faithful." (Hebrews 10:23)

Mom is the first person I called on Monday, July 5, 2010. Tearful and with a trembling voice, I told her that the Lord had done great things for me.[58] He had just split the Red Sea for me; He had opened a way where there was none. He had kept his promises. More than ever, I knew that I had to trust in God Eternal, against winds and tides. No mountain is too high for Him; no valley is too low for Him. He stands above all things.

For long minutes, I stared at my passport stamped with a long-stay student visa, as to make sure that I was not dreaming. My night dreams often took me to Europe, but on waking, I was always very disappointed, realizing that I was still in Abidjan. When the agent at the consulate gave me my visa then, I was not sure I was really awake. To confirm my waking state, I started jumping, screaming… crying tears of joy, a joy that only God can give.

---

[58] "Therefore I say to you, whatever things you ask when you pray, believe that you receive them, and you will have them." (Mark 11:24)

I went home with a heart full of gratitude. I was now staying with Gaston, another Christian friend. He believed my story, and had agreed to take me in until I left for France. At home, I burst into songs, all the songs that had so powerfully supported me in the darkest hours of this desert crossing. In particular, I hummed this song: "I know that You can do everything, and that nothing is impossible for You. Lord, make me see Your glory..."

The Lord had just made me see his glory! He had not been content with giving me a visa for France, but He had also provided a way to ensure my studies. As a matter of fact, when I informed the University of Nice of my absence from the first year exams, one of the program supervisors answered me: "That's all right. We can arrange a special exam session in a year for students who could not be present at the first year's session. That special session will be held during the week preceding the beginning of the second year exams in September 2011. You will have two weeks of exams then."

So I was still in the race for the master's in business administration! I blessed God Eternal, who knows all things, in advance: His ways are unfathomable. I had thought that all was lost, but I was discovering that God Eternal has the last word, always. My logic had led me to think that I had to get the visa before the exams, so that I could arrive in Nice on time. But God's logic is different. He had already foreseen an escape for me.[59] I decided that from then on, I would not panic at the slightest misgiving.

And it just happened that a number of misgivings still remained... I had not gathered the amount of money needed

---

[59] "And the LORD,
He is the One who goes before you.
He will be with you,
He will not leave you nor forsake you;
do not fear nor be dismayed." (Deuteronomy 31:8)

A Letter to God

for the plane ticket, but it did not bother me in the least. If God had granted me the student visa, and kept me in the race for the master's, then He certainly had already prepared the funding for the trip. My faith was revived.

Before the little congregation gathered around pastor Roger, I gave thanks to God for his blessings in my life. Everyone looked at me with admiration and respect, as if suddenly a halo had appeared around my head. After having aroused their pity for months, now I was envied by all these people. To them, my story manifested God's uplifting power. Does not humility precede glory? After having brought me down, God was now raising me up.[60] He was crowning me with the crown reserved for those who persevere to the end.[61]

In faith, I announced to the congregation that I was traveling the next day, July 7th. I was desperate to get to Nice before the end of the exams to have the opportunity to address certain financial and academic details. Nobody knew that I still did not have the money for the plane ticket. I had a total of $200.00 (100,000 FCFA) that one of my younger sisters had sent me a few days earlier. This left me with 24 hours to find $500.00 (250,000 FCFA).

The day of my scheduled flight, I visited Mr. Konan to bid him farewell. He had been a great blessing for me, and I wanted to thank him. He had been God's instrument in paying for the extension of my residence in Ivory Coast. God had turned to him when I was in need of a job. Mr. Konan was very moved by my tribute. As on the first day we met, he reached into his billfold and gave me $200.00 (100,000 FCFA). I only had $300.00 (150,000 FCFA) more to find.

That same day, Mom called me. She had managed to save a small part of the money she had received from the National

---

[60] "Therefore humble yourselves under the mighty hand of God, that He may exalt you in due time." (1 Peter 5:6)
[61] "For you have need of endurance, so that after you have done the will of God, you may receive the promise." (Hebrews 10:36)

Social Insurance Fund. Two weeks earlier, God had worked a miracle in our family: ten years after the suspension of her benefits, Mom had been reinstated in her rights. The CNPS[62] had refunded her the full amount of money she should have received from 2000 to 2010. She had received a lot of money unexpectedly.

In my opinion, this was not a coincidence. The happy ending of the financial conflict that had opposed my family to the Social Insurance Fund coincided with my student visa for France being granted. This case of suspension of benefits in 2000 had forced me to interrupt my studies. Ten years later, the resolution of that same case helped me to pay for the plane ticket to pursue my studies. When I tell you that nothing is impossible to God, and that all things work together for good to those who love Him...

The plane ticket paid for, I had no more to do than wait for the evening to get to the airport. I said goodbye to all my friends in Abidjan; their support had been precious during my times of trouble. I also announced the good news to my friends in other countries. Pierre, my friend from South Africa, was particularly moved. He congratulated me, and acknowledged that God's hand was with me. I had not been able to visit him, because my application to take part in the seminar in Johannesburg had been rejected. Pierre and I recognized that God had been behind this rejection. He had not allowed me to go to South Africa and live there illegally, because He had better to offer me. Thus, the Lord had delivered me from the temptation that could have ruined my chances of getting a student visa for France.

So God had denied the second request of my letter to grant the third, by far the most important. Just like for my failure at the radio station audition in 2002, I understood that any negative response from God always contributes to our

---

[62] French acronym, *Caisse nationale de prévoyance sociale*.

well being:[63] either what we ask God is right, but the time to receive it is not, or what we ask God is contrary to his plans, and He does not grant it. In this case, the Johannesburg seminar had been a trap set by the enemy to distract me from God's plan.

Christian accompanied me to the Abidjan International Airport. He could well understand the emotion that subdued me. The homeless man he had rescued was about to fly to the Promised Land, the land flowing with milk and honey: " ... Europe, Europe."

---

[63] "And we know that all things work together for good to those who love God..." (Romans 8:28)

CHAPTER 15

The Promised Land

"Blessed is the man who endures temptation; for when he has been approved, he will receive the crown of life which the Lord has promised to those who love Him." (James 1:12)

I couldn't believe my eyes! The Mediterranean Sea, lapping at my feet, shined brilliantly. I had read about this sea in geography books, unaware that some day, I would be on familiar terms with it. I was standing on the beach in Nice... I was on the French Riviera! The beach was packed with people, vacationers from around the world, for the most part, rich people who had the means to afford the luxury of the Riviera under the summer sun. They must have thought that I belonged to their social class, probably the son of a wealthy African dignitary who had come to sample the delights of *La promenade des Anglais*, but I was more than that: I was the son[64] of the Living God, who sits the poor at the table of the rich.[65]

---

64   "For as many as are led by the Spirit of God, these are sons of God." (Romans 8:14)
65   "He raises the poor from the dust
     And lifts the beggar from the ash heap,
     To set them among princes
     And make them inherit the throne of glory..." (1 Samuel 2:8)

Twenty-four hours earlier, I was still homeless in Abidjan. In just a brief moment, God had pulled me from the depths of misery, and dropped me in the middle of the most luxurious tourism spot of Europe. I was not sulking, but found pleasure in this vacation scene that provided consolation for my troubles. God knows how to procure rest to afflicted souls.[66] In times of affliction, He promises not to leave us, not to abandon us. He had just demonstrated it in my life, including since my arrival in France.

On Thursday night, I had checked into a hotel in Nice. The next day, I went to the University of Nice. As I wanted to address the tuition payment issue, I was referred to the accounts department of the university, somewhere else in Nice; I got lost on the way. So I approached a car at a red light to ask for information. Before I got the chance to say a word, the driver opened the car door and invited me in.

His name was Ibrahim, a young Mauritanian. He had been in France for three years, and he, too, was a student at the University of Nice. He drove me to the university's accounts department. When I introduced myself to the accounting officer, he readily identified me... my file had been the object of many legal proceedings. Nicole had been ordered by a bailiff to pay my tuition fees. As she was not able to do so, the case was about to be sent to trial. Poor Nicole! She had been under heavy pressure on my account.

I asked the accounting officer to discharge Nicole of all liability. Now that I was in France, I could be responsible for my own affairs. I had to sign a letter of acknowledgement of debt to the university, as well as a commitment form to settle this debt prior to the resumption of the second year, in September 2010. This meant that I had to pay the total sum of $4,000.00 for the first year to be able to enroll in the second year of the master's. As for the tuition of the second

---

[66] "Come to Me, all you who labor and are heavy laden, and I will give you rest." (Matthew 11:28)

year, another $4,000.00, I could settle it through bimonthly payments, beginning in February 2011.

I breathed a big sigh of relief! The worst had just been avoided. Nicole was out of trouble. As for me, I now had two months to come up with $4,000.00. Of course I had no idea where to start to find so much money in such a short time; but God Eternal knew for sure. He had not brought me this far simply to abandon me. When He begins something, He sees it through.

Ibrahim offered me a meal at McDonald's in the city center. It was my first taste of *fast food*, western style. I shared my story with Ibrahim, told him how good God had been to me. He seemed to be interested, despite the theological divide between Muslims and Christians. At the end of the meal, he gave me tips on finding a job in France: things to do and things to avoid. At some point, I realized that Ibrahim had dedicated most of his day to me. Many hours had run by since I had hopped in his car till the meal at the restaurant. I left him with the promise that I'd see him the next day, and I headed out to the beach.

I was still in awe in front of this splendid seaside setting, aware that God followed me everywhere. The same God who had saved me through his powerful hand in Cotonou and Abidjan had just placed Ibrahim on my path. Ibrahim had showed no hesitation at helping a stranger by giving him time and money. This kindness of God towards me, it seemed at that moment, found its perfect symbol in the rolling motion of the waves: there are times in life when one is in the trough of the wave, and other times when the blessings[67] of the Eternal One wash over us like waves…

Saturday, July 10th, Ibrahim joined me at the station in Nice. I was going to Nancy, where my older brother, Albert, had been living for twenty-two years. Two years before the

---

67   "The blessing of the Lord makes one rich,
And He adds no sorrow with it." (Proverbs 10:22)

A Letter to God

death of our father, he had obtained a scholarship in France. I was eager to join him; I had not seen him for many years. Also, he had helped me create my file for a long-stay student visa. Especially, he had vouched for my accommodation in France during the first months of my stay.

I stood in a stupor before the wicket: the ticket between Nice and Nancy cost $136.00; I was $27.00 short. Ibrahim, seeing my pain, took the money from his wallet and handed it to me. Certainly God had placed him on my path to bless me at the beginning of my adventure on French soil.

On the train, I sat next to a young man. I was hungry. I had skipped breakfast for lack of money, so I had no energy. Coincidentally, as my hunger became more pressing, the young man sitting next to me chose to buy a sandwich and a can of juice. I prayed in my heart... "Lord, I pray: touch this young man's heart so that he shares with me his sandwich and his juice. In the name of Jesus Christ. Amen." The minute I said "Amen," the young man turned to me and offered me his sandwich. He also gave me his can of juice... Never before had I experienced such a quick response to my prayer.[68] Certainly, I had just established a world record: a prayer granted in less than a second! This experience showed me how much God cared about my needs, down to the smallest details. I was his child, and I depended on Him for everything, including breakfast. In God's eyes, there's no shameful prayer.[69]

---

[68] "And whatever things you ask in prayer, believing, you will receive." (Matthew 21:22)
[69] "The LORD is near to all who call upon Him,
To all who call upon Him in truth." (Psalms 145:18)

Chapter 16

Under the Stars

*"I will both lie down in peace, and sleep;
For You alone, O Lord, make me dwell in safety."
(Psalms 4:8)*

I strolled the streets of Paris that night, my very first visit to the City of Lights... and light was abundant. I was awestruck! As I reached the height of Saint-Lazare in the 8th arrondissement, I saw a fast food restaurant. I noticed the security guard inside. I went to him, and asked how one could become a security guard in France. It was complicated: one first has to receive the required training before applying for the job. Seeing my determination to work in just about anything, the guard suggested I submit my application to the manager of the restaurant.

I resumed my wanderings in the City of Lights. I walked aimlessly, letting my instinct guide me: when I arrived at a street corner, I looked all around and continued in the direction that seemed the most beautiful. More than anything else, I just wanted to pass the time, because I had nowhere to sleep. I tried not to worry about it, simply admiring the nocturnal beauty of Paris.

I carried extra clothes and my résumé with cover letters in a small knapsack. I had left the rest of my belongings with

Anita, a friend I had met on a social networking site when I was in Nancy. She lived in Argenteuil, a suburb of Paris. Through a mutual friend, she had befriended me on the site. So when it was time for me to leave Nancy, I had asked Anita the favor to keep my bags in her place for a few days. I had not asked her to lodge me: it was our first time to meet, so I did not want to abuse her generosity.

Alone in the streets of Paris, I could not help but think of the family comfort I had found with my older brother in Nancy. His family had offered me a warm welcome. Albert lived in the suburbs, in a quiet village where life was good. Sometimes, I took a walk in nature. Other times, I went biking along the river. During those moments of spiritual recreation, I renewed my commitment to serve God, to remain faithful to Him, to obey Him in all things and to let Him guide my life. Considering all that I had been through till then, I understood that it was in my best interest to let God guide me, and make me the person He wanted me to be.[70]

For a month and a half, I had had a wonderful vacation in Nancy. Between excursions in the forest, hiking, picnicking, swimming, bike rides, walks in the city and fireworks on July 14th, it had been by far the best vacation of my life. All the days had been equally beautiful; my happiness had been constant. No song of praise was too much to express my gratitude to the Lord who had brought me to Europe. He never ceased to amaze me.

One day, I went to a shoe store with Valerie, my brother's wife. She had given me clothes a few days earlier, and now wanted me to discover the shoe stores in Nancy. In one of the stores, Valerie recognized a friend who was about to buy a pair of sneakers. When he saw me, he realized that I needed

---

[70] "Before I formed you in the womb I knew you;
Before you were born I sanctified you;
I ordained you a prophet to the nations." (Jeremiah 1:5)

a new pair of shoes. He offered me the pair he was wearing, and then put on the new pair he had just purchased.

Since I had arrived in France, the Lord had constantly blessed me through strangers: Ibrahim in Nice, the young man on the train and now Valerie's friend. I remembered that in Abidjan, I myself had graciously offered my clothes and a pair of shoes to Christian. Was the Lord trying to reward my generosity? Whatever, I knew that he who gives receives also.[71] The church had taught me.

Life was pleasant in Nancy, but I could not find either an internship or a part-time job. The city had only a few jobs to offer, and many students to cover them. It was difficult for me to land anything. I began to search for jobs and internships all through France via Internet. A company in Paris contacted me.

The company offered in-home services: housekeeping and ironing. I had applied for an internship in human resources within that small business. When I was contacted for an interview, I took the opportunity to pack up my suitcases. I was ready to leave Nancy to go to Paris, where employment opportunities were better. I had a good reason: a sword of Damocles was still hanging over my head. The deadline for the payment of $4,000.00 to the university was coming close, and I still had not found work. I was aware that the interview in Paris would not necessarily lead to an internship, and that I was undertaking a risky venture because I had no place to stay in Paris, but my decision was made. I had to go at all costs.

It was cold that night in Paris, and I continued my wanderings in the night, undoubtedly guided by the Holy Spirit. I arrived at a street corner flooded with light: a wide, well-lit avenue, lined with immaculately trimmed trees and flowers.

---

[71] "Give, and it will be given to you: good measure, pressed down, shaken together, and running over will be put into your bosom. For with the same measure that you use, it will be measured back to you." (Luke 6:38)

A Letter to God

I was not alone on the street, although it was late in the night. Most department stores located on both sides of the avenue were still open. I felt a boost of energy: I was on the Avenue des Champs-Élysées! I had often heard on television that it was the most beautiful avenue in the world. That evening, my amazement confirmed that reputation. I, too, could now boast of having been to the Avenue des Champs-Élysées. I was on a cloud! A moment later, I got off my cloud; reality was cruel: amid the luxury and the joyful honking, I was lonely and homeless.

I randomly walked to Avenue Foch nearby. There, I noticed an entrance to an underground parking lot. I entered, hoping to find a refuge. The heat in the underground parking contrasted with the severe cold outside. I had to take my clothes off to avoid death by asphyxiation. That was my first night in Paris.

In the early morning, I set out to explore the French capital. Using a map, I visited on foot a few touristic landmarks: the Arc de triomphe, the Place de la Concorde, the Tuileries Garden, the Louvre Museum, the Tour Montparnasse and, of course, the Eiffel Tower. In one day, I visited Paris without any tour guide.

In the evening, I returned home in the prestigious 16th arrondissement of Paris, in this luxurious underground apartment I had found the night before on Avenue Foch. I was truly grateful to God for that *warm* place He had reserved for me. During my exploration of Paris, I had seen other homeless persons lying on the streets, shivering with cold. At least I had a warm hiding place, and more, in a renowned district.

In the middle of my sleep, I was brutally awakened by a dog barking in my face: a few inches only separated our eyes; I could have sworn that the beast was only waiting for his master's orders to pounce on me. With a voice as firm as it was pitiless, the security guard ordered me to clear off: "It is not allowed to sleep here. Go away." I got dressed as the dog kept his cruel stare on me. Still in shock, I wondered why the guard needed a dog to chase away a homeless and helpless person.

Outside, the ruthless cold air hit me like a brick; I had never felt so cold in all my life. I had just arrived in Europe, used to life in the tropics of Africa. For a moment, I lay down on one of the benches in the Avenue des Champs-Élysées, but after fifteen minutes, I realized that I would not survive through this glacial cold. I set out to look for a metro station. I found Line 1 of the Paris Metro. Even after midnight, the last metro trains were still running. I climbed in one of them, not caring where it went. After several minutes, I heard: "Château de Vincennes." I had arrived at the end of the line. I got out and climbed into the train going in the opposite direction, La Défense.

The splendor of La Défense, Paris's business district, dazzled me. The bright lights of the skyscrapers and the twinkling stars higher up offered me an incredible show. I had my head in the stars, but I could not afford to be distracted for too long. It was important that I hit the ground again, or rather the underground, where I was hoping to find shelter from the cold. I spotted a small area, a kind of public toilet that served as my dormitory for the night.

I woke up quite stiff the next day. My body was aching. I had slept on the ground two nights in a row: it was too much! Nonetheless, I did not feel abandoned by God. On the opposite, I thanked him for having protected me during those two nights.[72] In addition, I was sensitive to the beauty of the places where God Eternal had led me: the Avenue des Champs-Élysées, the Avenue Foch, La Défense. I felt privileged, as if I belonged to a higher social class: the class of luxury homelessness! These opulent neighborhoods were perhaps the premonition of my glorious destiny. One day, I

---

72   "For He shall give His angels charge over you,
To keep you in all your ways." (Psalms 91:11)

would live on Avenue Foch for real, and I would work in the district of La Défense for real...

CHAPTER 17

In the Shelter of the Most High

"He who dwells in the secret place of the Most High Shall abide under the shadow of the Almighty." (Psalms 91:1)

On my knees, next to the bed in my hotel room, I wept profusely. Since the Lord had enrolled me in his school of faith, my tears had become the expression of my gratitude for his marvelous deeds in my life. Here I was in this hotel room, graciously offered to me after two nights on the street. I had finally found a comfortable refuge in a city where I knew no one.

After my second night on the street, I had prayed to God: "Lord, I am exhausted. I don't want to spend a third night outside. Please, find me lodging today. In faith, I welcome my place of accommodation in the name of Jesus Christ. Amen." I had prayed unto God, as a child to his father. In my mind, there had not been a shadow of a doubt that the Lord would grant my prayer.

As I woke up the next morning, a Sunday morning, I remembered that I had seen an evangelical church on my way to drop my bags at Anita's apartment. So I took the bus, and went to the Evangelical Church of Argenteuil.

At the end of the service, I explained my situation to a church official. I told him that I wanted to be hosted temporarily by a member of the church, until I found my own housing. Indeed, I had the financial means to rent an apartment. Shortly before leaving Nancy, I had opened a bank account. The client advisor at the bank had suggested that I take a student loan of $1,300.00 without interest, refundable over twelve months, which I had hurried to accept. The money had already been transferred to my account, although I did not yet have a credit card or a checkbook to access it.

The support group of the Evangelical Church of Argenteuil welcomed me warmly. Caroline and her husband were appointed to give me all the support I needed. At first, they advised me to call 115, a local number providing assistance to the homeless in need of temporary shelter. As there was no space available in the temporary residences, Caroline and her husband found me a hotel room in Argenteuil, paid by the church.

I stayed at the hotel for a few days, then the good news finally arrived: a brother in Christ from the church had agreed to accommodate me temporarily. I rejoiced at the news, and could not help but draw a parallel between this act of kindness and what I had experienced in Abidjan. The pastor in Abidjan had refused to enlist the help of the faithful, under the pretext that I had been attending the church for a few weeks only. I had been left to my fate, because the church members did not know me. Here, at the Evangelical Church of Argenteuil, nobody had raised thousands of questions about me. On the very first day, a hotel room had graciously been offered to the stranger that I was; and the church had taken the risk of asking one of its members to lodge a stranger, someone who had landed from nowhere. I had experienced two places, two churches... two different visions of charity.

Henry welcomed me in his home in Argenteuil. He was going through hard times in his personal and spiritual life.

After I told him my story from Cotonou to Paris, he prayed aloud: "Lord, I am sorry that I have shunned you because of my problems. I thought that I was the most miserable man on earth, but listening to Antoine's story, I realize that you have always given me everything. I could never have borne a tenth of what Antoine has endured... It is true that you send trials to each, according to his capacity. Antoine was able to resist, I could never have."

Henry took care of me. He shared his food and lodging, without asking anything in return. During my stay with him, I found my first job in France. The restaurant in Saint-Lazare had finally hired me to work part-time. I was making burgers. Strong with this new job and with the loan money I had in the bank, I started to look for an apartment.

I discovered my apartment in Moissy-Cramayel, a town about thirty minutes from Paris, in a boarding house for students. Laurence, the owner, lived there herself. Each year, she carefully selected three students to whom she rented a room. When I found this house, I knew inside that the Lord had kept this place for me.

The first time I saw Laurence and her house, I met a young Ivorian student who had stayed there the previous year. He was moving to Évry, south of Paris, to get closer to his university. The young man stared at me and then, joyfully, exclaimed: "Are you not a television reporter? I think I used to see your face on TV when I lived in Abidjan." Definitely, God Eternal had planned everything, to the point of leading me to meet, in this house in France, someone from Ivory Coast who had seen me as a reporter on television. This meeting with this young Ivorian echoed in my mind as confirmation that I was in the right place. Laurence also was pleasantly surprised, and her decision to accept me in was the logical consequence.

I moved in my new room at the end of September. Since I mentioned my faith in Jesus Christ from time to time,

Laurence told me about her doctor who shared the same beliefs. It's no surprise that I chose that doctor later when the Public Social Security Service asked me to elect a doctor.

Dr. Chantal advised me to join an evangelical church not far from Moissy-Cramayel. In a few days, the church choir was presenting a gospel music concert. The opportunity was therefore conducive to experience the atmosphere of the church before making a decision.

The concert was presented on November 26th. I saw snow for the first time in my life that day. The coincidence was probably not trivial... The gospel music concert was a magical moment! The following Sunday, I went to that church. From the start of the service, I was convinced in my heart that I was in the right place: I had found my church in France.

CHAPTER 18

Between the Hammer and the Anvil

*"I will lift up my eyes to the hills—
From whence comes my help?
My help comes from the Lord,
Who made heaven and earth."
(Psalms 121:1-2)*

The deadline for the payment of the first year university had expired. I had not been able to honor my commitment to pay the required $4,000.00 before the beginning of the second year. All of a sudden, I found myself in a tight spot: the accounting department of the University of Nice had contacted me several times, and threatened to submit my case to the court. Moreover, I did not have access to the online training platform anymore. Having been unable to renew my registration for the second year of the master's program, I could not access the courses on-line.

I had serious financial troubles. My monthly income of $700.00 from the restaurant paid for the $500.00 rent. The remaining $200.00 did not cover the other basic needs: health, nutrition, commute and telephone. I was desperately looking for a paid internship to get back in the saddle. My student status in France allowed me to combine work and training. So I was determined to find a paid internship during the day, while preserving my weekly sixteen hours of work during the evening.

I had been looking for an internship for a long time, without success. The small business offering in-home services had not accepted my application for the internship in human resources. Since then, I had had several interviews with other companies, but each time I had not been accepted. One director of an event-planning firm in Paris had shown interest in my profile, but she wondered if I could write French correctly. "If the French themselves make grammar and spelling mistakes when they write, what will it be with you who have studied French in Africa?" I had to smile inside; her comment demonstrated her lack of general culture regarding French in Africa.

As the end of the year was getting close, the intensity of my stress was increasing. I did not want to start 2011 without a positive outlook for my studies. I absolutely had to find an internship before the end of the year. Tired of failing with the small- and medium-sized enterprises, I decided to turn to the bigger companies. I went to the business district of La Défense, where the largest companies in France are located. One of them specifically caught my attention.

At first, I was intimidated; the imposing skyscraper that stood before me was impressive to say the least: a bright, luminous, stunning building. I told myself that I could never get an internship in this type of company: *Certainly internships here are reserved for students of high social rank; even for a middle class French person, it would be difficult to be accepted, more so for me, newly arrived in France.* As I pondered this, I remembered my status in Jesus Christ: I am the son of the living God, who sits the poor at the table of the rich. Energized by this thought, I entered the building, and obtained all the information I needed to submit my application.

A few days later, during the last week of the year, I received an invitation to an interview from three separate departments of that same company. I attended three interviews, and was selected as an intern by one of the departments. The company even gave me the luxury of setting the duration of my internship. As my goal was to pay for my studies, I chose a long internship of twelve months in order to earn the most money.

The start date of my internship was set for January 2011. In one week, the Lord had given me the paid internship I had so desired since my arrival in France. I realized that time is not a limit for God.[73] When his time of blessing comes, He makes us complete in one day what would have taken years to achieve.

I was also impressed by the location of my internship, La Défense, this business district where I had slept in an underground toilet on my second night in Paris. From the depths of the basement of La Défense, I had been propelled to the top of the skyscrapers: the social elevator ride that God gave me by this internship was amazing.[74]

Although the university had not yet signed my internship agreement, my host company admitted me in training on January 17, 2011. Both the university and the host company should sign this legal document before the actual start of the training. In my case, the internship agreement had been signed by the company and mailed to the university. As it waited for the university's response, the human resources department of the company had let me begin the internship. God's favor continued to flow abundantly in my life.

---

[73] "The Lord is not slack concerning His promise, as some count slackness, but is longsuffering toward us, not willing that any should perish but that all should come to repentance." (2 Peter 3:9)
[74] "Humble yourselves in the sight of the Lord, and He will lift you up." (James 4:10)

After one week, the university still had not responded. The internship advisor at the university explained that the agreement could not be signed until I paid the full amount of $4,000,00, for the first year of the master's program. At the same time, the human resources department of the company insisted that I find a solution to this problem within two days. Otherwise, my internship would be canceled.

So I was stuck between the hammer and the anvil: the university demanded $4,000.00 right away, and the company would not keep a student who was not in good standing. After such a struggle, I had just obtained an internship that triggered much hope: it gave me the means to write my dissertation, and thus complete the master's program; it was also the answer to the funding of my studies. It guaranteed me an income of $1,300.00 a month, which was sufficient to gradually pay for the entire master's program that cost a total of $8,000.00. If I could not continue this internship, I would not even be able to settle the debt of $4,000.00 for the first year already completed.

I proposed to the university that I pay for the whole program by installments. I was ready to pay the sum of $1,600.00 bimonthly, starting in February 2011, which meant that I would complete the payment of $8,000.00 in October 2011, but the university presented a flat refusal to my proposal. It remained firm in its request that I pay $4,000.00 total before I could begin to pay the next $4,000.00 by installments for the second year. I was given forty-eight hours to find this money.

The stakes were high; the pressure was unbearable... I was panicking! Where to turn to find such a sum of money? I could not concentrate at my work anymore; the ultimatum of the human resources department preoccupied me. I was on the verge of losing an internship that I had struggled so much to get: I had spent no less than two hours on telephone interviews with recruiters of the company, following which three departments of the company had contacted me for an interview in person.

I turned to God; gold and silver belong to him.[75] I prayed the famous "Psalm 23" that had supported me so well during my journey through the desert while I was in Africa. This psalm has an extraordinary power: it lifts my faith, and leads me to consider any new problem as an additional opportunity for God to manifest his power.

The day before the expiration of the ultimatum presented by my hosting company, I received a call from the University of Nice. The internship advisor informed me that the director of the institution had finally agreed to sign my internship agreement, despite the fact that I still had not paid the required $4,000.00. To reassure my hosting company, the university had sent a scanned copy of the internship agreement to the Department of Human Resources by e-mail. "However," continued the advisor, "the original agreement will be sent to your business only after you have paid, in full, the $4,000.00 for the first year of your master's."

Once again, God had intervened masterfully in my life. He had changed the attitude of the directors of the university. They had relented and agreed to sign the agreement. The sword of Damocles that hung over my head was momentarily taken away. The company let me continue my internship, while reserving the right to terminate it at any time if the original agreement was not received. So I had more time to find $4,000.00.

I was not completely in the clear. As usual, I lifted my eyes to the heavens to implore the help of God.[76] He certainly had already reserved the money for my studies somewhere;

---

[75] "'The silver is Mine, and the gold is Mine,' says the LORD of hosts." (Haggai 2:8)
[76] "I will lift up my eyes to the hills—
From whence comes my help?
My help comes from the Lord,
Who made heaven and earth." (Psalms 121:1-2)

all that remained for me was to discover where. The Spirit of God put into my heart the thought of explaining my situation to Junior, a friend who attended the Firm Founders International Ministries (FFIM) Church with me. Junior offered to talk to the pastor of the church.

I suggested that they give me a loan, but I was not sure that my request was acceptable. Indeed, it was not obvious that the small church would have $4,000.00 readily available. And in the event that the money was available, it was still necessary that the church agree to loan money to a stranger. I had been attending the FFIM Church for two months only; I was still a stranger to the pastor. I feared that he would not trust me... as had been my experience in Abidjan.

After a few days, Junior told me the good news: the Pastor had agreed to give me a loan of $4,000.00 on behalf of the church. I was rescued! The Lord had solved my problem in a way that I had not considered when I was in Abidjan. Really, when I had made that request in my letter to God, I never thought in a thousand years that the answer would come through a community church... the great family of Christ. What I needed, the Lord had kept in his house for me.

Some time later, my hosting company received the original internship agreement, and I was confirmed as an intern. So God, my God, had been in control of the situation from the beginning: He had just confirmed my internship in this multinational enterprise. It was exactly what I had asked my God in my letter in Abidjan. Furthermore, thanks to $1,300.00 that I would receive every month for my internship allowance, the financing of my studies was provided: Jehovah-jireh had provided.[77]

---

77 "And Abraham called the name of that place Jehovah-jireh. As it is said to this day, In the mount of Jehovah it shall be provided." (Genesis 22:14). American Standard Version (1901).

CHAPTER 19

Face To Face

"And you shall know the truth, and the truth shall make you free." (John 8:32)

The rendezvous with Nicole had been set for the afternoon. Since I had arrived in France, I had not had the courage to call her... to face her. I had sent her a message, shortly after my arrival, informing her that she was free from prosecution. That's all I was capable of then. I dreaded the meeting. It could turn volatile: I had caused Nicole unexpected legal troubles; I had deprived her of the money she had saved for her own studies. I could imagine her disappointment and her anger towards me.

Of course, I had apologized many times when I was still living in Benin; I had asked her forgiveness for all the harm I had caused. I was still well aware that mere words were not enough to appease her fury. Surely, our friendship was broken. I had suggested this rendezvous, hoping we could pick up the pieces together. I intended to tell her my story, the story of my descent into hell, tell her everything I had endured in Cotonou, Abidjan and Paris, tell her that I had been without any resources at all, regarding her legitimate demand that I pay back the $600.00, tell her that I had no control over the situation, tell her finally how sorry I was...

A Letter to God

We planned to meet in the restaurant where I worked at Saint-Lazare in Paris. When I saw Nicole walking towards me, I became very emotional. I had not seen her for six years. Under normal circumstances, we would have embraced, shown excitement, in memory of the good old days, but now the context was different. This was not a reunion between longtime friends, but rather a clarification meeting between a victim and her executioner. At least, that's how I viewed it.

The greetings were simple and polite, not warm, not cold, but when I began to speak, the atmosphere immediately relaxed as if by magic. In a moment, we found that complicity that had brought us together in the past. It was as if Nicole and I had been born to get along! Listening to my story, she was overwhelmed with emotions, perceiving the pain I had endured during this long ordeal. She was so moved that she apologized for the mental harassment she had put me through in her hope that I would pay her back. This was the world upside down! I had come to ask Nicole to forgive me for all that she had suffered because of me, but surprisingly, it was she who was apologizing to me...

She told me what had happened on her side all this time: indeed, she had struggled to enroll in her university program, but something extraordinary had happened. Her school had granted her a period of several months to pay the required sum, a unique favor of its kind, as only God knows how to provide them. Like me, Nicole had found excellent opportunities for internships and jobs that had allowed her to pay her debt to the school. These opportunities that she had taken advantage of were nothing less than a rainfall of blessings that God Eternal had poured in her life.

I was convinced now that God had not abandoned Nicole. Although I had not been able to repay my debt at the right time, God had seen to it that Nicole's studies would not be negatively affected. He had provided for her beyond my expectations... Even the contentious bank account that Nicole had opened so that I could pay the university by installments had become a blessing for her later on. She explained that the bank account she had shared with her husband had been closed, following their marital break-up. So she had used the bank account that was supposed to finance my studies.

God's ways are truly unpredictable: a serious problem for Nicole in the beginning had become the solution for another problem.[78] I understood then that God had chosen to bless me with this friend, because He had prepared for her also a path of blessings in anticipation of her personal hardships. I paid my debt of $600.00, and Nicole was delighted.

All the questions I had asked in Cotonou had found their answer: God was a just God; He had not favored me at Nicole's expense; He had granted Nicole the means to finance her studies; He had taken care of her in difficult times... When I was in Cotonou, I wondered why the Lord had let the storm strike at my relationship with Nicole, but now I could see the benefits that storm had carried. Certainly, each of us had suffered, but in the end, my relationship with Nicole had come out stronger than ever. God had safeguarded our friendship; better, he had strengthened it.

---

[78] "Better is the end of a thing than the beginning thereof..." (Ecclesiastes 7:8)

Chapter 20

The Hour of Truth

"Better is the end of a thing than the beginning thereof..." (Ecclesiastes 7:8)

I no longer believed that I would ever get my Master in Business Administration. The exam session was fast approaching, and I was not ready at all. Not only did I have close to twenty classes to review, but I also had a dissertation to write. The workload was such that I had no chance to prepare seriously for the exams in September 2011. A certain failure loomed on the horizon. How did I get here?

I had experienced very difficult times since the beginning of 2011, since I had started my internship. I spent my days and my nights working tirelessly. During the day, I worked as an intern at La Défense from 9 A.M. to 5 P.M. In the evening, I worked at the restaurant from 7 P.M. to midnight. This was the price to pay just to make ends meet, to finance my personal needs and my studies. On one hand, I had to pay rent, food, transport and other bills; on the other hand, I still had the $8,000.00 debt to the university. I was gradually paying the $4,000.00 the church had lent me; I was also paying the $4,000.00 to the university, by installments, for my second year of the master's.

The Hour of Truth

My daily routine was infernal: I finished my work at the restaurant at midnight, and then took the metro and a commuter train to get home in Moissy-Cramayel. Since the night trains were far apart, I usually got home by 1:15 A.M. Then I still had to walk twenty minutes in the cold, because the buses had stopped running. Exhausted, I crawled in bed at around 2 A.M., aware that my sleep would be very short.

Waking up was painful, more so than what I had experienced as a child when Mom woke me up at dawn to fetch water at the spring. My mind was willing to make it to La Défense for 9 A.M., but my body was begging for more sleep. It was obvious that five hours of sleep were not enough to recover from all the work I was doing day and night. At 7 A.M., when the alarm went off, all my muscles still felt the fatigue of the previous day. Once aboard the train to La Défense, I tried somehow to catch up on my sleep.

Under such conditions, the beginning of my internship could only be strenuous. I lacked liveliness and concentration. Sometimes, at work, sleep demanded that I pay back the hours I had denied it. Its orders were pressing, and hardly left me any choice: I had to obey the call to sleep! Rumors circulated within the company: an intern was sleeping during working hours. One day, a supervisor found me asleep. He informed my internship advisor, who gave me extra work to keep me busy.

With such a pace at work, I had no time left to study. I had already given up ages ago. Only two months before the exams, I fully realized the urgency of my situation, more so since I still had not caught up with the courses between September 2010 and February 2011. During that period, I had not had access to the on-line training platform, because I had not paid the required fees. I had to act fast if I still wanted a chance at my degree.

Towards the end of July, I decided to end my work at the restaurant. So I had a little more time to devote to my exams, but obviously it was a bit late to catch up. Until then, my involvement with the second year courses had been rather superficial. I had not submitted much of the homework; I had a dissertation to write on a theme that was still not set... I was out of step with the plans of the Lord for me about the master's program.

The possibility of failure stressed me more and more. The Lord had invested in this master's and was committed to it. He had miraculously facilitated my registration at the last minute; He had taken me to France to continue my studies; He had given me a paid internship that allowed me to fund the master's. And yet, I was about to disappoint Him. All the sacrifices and the hardships endured would therefore have been useless. Sometimes, I thought that God would understand this failure: He was, himself, a witness to the hardships of my life; He knew that I was working extra hard just to survive and to pay for my studies; He saw my fatigue. At the same time, I felt guilty for having let the means become more important than the goal: I had been so concerned with the funding of my studies that I had put the studies themselves aside.

However, I relied on the grace and mercy of God. Despite my lack of preparation, He was able to carry out a prowess. He had already done it in the past, when He had shown me in advance the mathematics and chemistry questions on the high school exam. I only had to concentrate on my share of the responsibility. As much as it was possible, I had to work twice as hard to make up for the time lost; I had to stand tall and face the challenge of the exams with courage and determination. After all that, then I would be entitled to ask God Eternal for help.[79]

---

[79] "For the eyes of the L ORD run to and fro throughout the whole earth, to show Himself strong on behalf of those whose heart is loyal to Him. In this you have done foolishly; therefore from now on you shall have wars." (2 Chronicles 16:9)

So I went to Nice, determined to succeed at my exams: the story had to have a good ending; I had to obtain the master's degree. I was welcomed in Nice in a family I had befriended. A few months earlier, my older sister had put me in touch with Alex, a friend of her friend, who lived in Nice. Alex and I had become friends; he was putting me up now for the exams session. At his place, I spent two weeks in a studious atmosphere. The first week, I had to do the exams of the first year. I had missed them in July 2010. The second week, I had the exams of the second year, with the defense of my dissertation as the very last part. At the end of each day of exams, I spent the whole night to review the subjects for the next day. So it was throughout the entire exams session.

I returned to Paris somewhat optimistic: I had fought well! Apart from the exams on "Cost Analysis and Management Control" and on "Budget Management", which had given me cold sweats, the other exams had not been too difficult. Ultimately, my hopes of obtaining the master's were high. Of course, I remained realistic! I knew full well that I would not get this degree with a mention, except "Passed," of course. And if my grade was below the average of 10/20, I still had a second chance available. *After all, a degree is a degree,* I told myself, *with or without a mention. It does not matter!*

In December, I returned to Nice for the big day, graduation day. I was part of the graduating class of 2011 in the Master of Business Administration program. These studies that God had so prodigiously begun in Cotonou were about to find their best conclusion. Not only had I obtained my master's, but I did with the honor befitting a child of God: I got a mention! The grade of 12/20 was totally unexpected, given my preparation. God had acted beyond my expectations.

I thanked the Lord for this triumphal ending, the culmination of a long journey that had taken place in three countries,

A Letter to God

and that had seriously tested my faith.[80] Already in Cotonou, when I did not even have enough to eat, I had believed in this studies project that would cost $12,000.00. I had been content with believing in God Eternal and his words, without paying attention to my current condition.

That day in Nice, holding my diploma in hand, I had to admit that my condition had changed since my departure from Cotonou, even physically. The weakling I had been in Benin had become a man of good stature. I was grateful to God who had fed me, protected me and kept me in good health, despite adversity. I had expressed that need in my letter in Abidjan, and God had responded favorably.

Back in Moissy-Cramayel, I kept rehashing the words the guest speaker had spoken at the graduation ceremony in Nice. He said that we were part of this batch of young entrepreneurs who have the world within reach. "Do not limit yourself to France," he had said, "go, and see what's happening elsewhere in the world, in the United States for example. Do business wherever opportunities arise." The Lord had guided me to the master's to make me an entrepreneur, a businessman, who would work at the advancement of the Kingdom of God. That was the meaning of the visions of Cotonou. Beyond Africa and Europe, my mission field had expanded to the entire world.

---

[80] "In this you greatly rejoice, though now for a little while, if need be, you have been grieved by various trials, that the genuineness of your faith, being much more precious than gold that perishes, though it is tested by fire, may be found to praise, honor, and glory at the revelation of Jesus Christ." (1 Peter 1:6-7)

The Hour of Truth

Graduation ceremony in Nice, December 2011.

Chapter 21

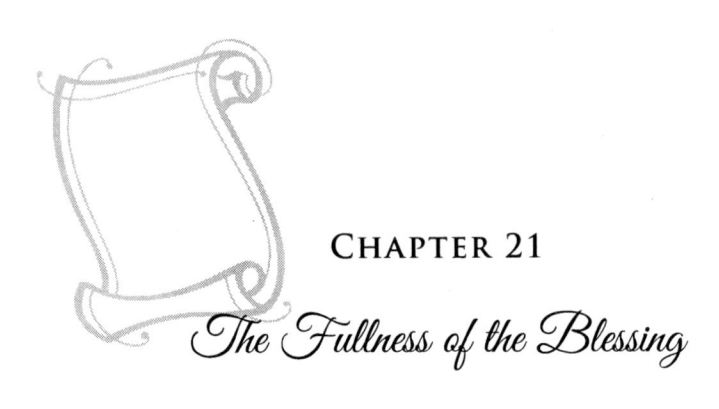

The Fullness of the Blessing

"The blessing of the Lord makes one rich, And He adds no sorrow with it." (Proverbs 10:22)

In the vehicle that was taking me to the Roissy-Charles-de-Gaulle airport on the morning of July 3, 2012, I could not hide my concern. The young woman at the wheel was lost. Natasha could not remember the way to the airport. We were lost in Paris! I did not know what to do, not knowing the way myself. During my stay in Paris without a car, I had not learned to know the city so well. Given my precarious situation, I could not afford the luxury of a vehicle. However, I was well acquainted with the metro lines and the trains.

Natasha had insisted to drive me to the airport; it would add beauty to the departure. She had not wanted that we get caught in the crowds on public transportation. The idea was rather generous, except that Natasha had not thought that she might get lost on the way. I checked my watch constantly; my departure time was close. I could not afford to miss my flight; I would lose my plane ticket: I had bought a low-cost non-refundable ticket. But there was worse to fear; my whole future was at stake. Indeed, my residence on French soil expired two days later, on July 5th. If I missed this flight,

I ran the risk of becoming an illegal resident in France, which would compromise my travel plans. Natasha was aware of this; it added to her stress.

I had met Natasha for the first time in November 2010, at the gospel concert that had made me discover the Firm Founders International Ministries Church. Later, we took the habit of exchanging a few words of courtesy at the end of each service, but it is on board commuter trains that our friendship really found its pace. One day, on my way to my internship company, I met Natasha on the train. The next day, at the same time, I met her again on the same train. She was going to school in Paris every morning.

The train became a favored meeting place for us. We learned to know each other. She had a sweet character and a sensitive heart. Her presentation was surprisingly simple, which allowed me to focus on her character rather than on her physical beauty. I needed to work on that. In Cameroon, I had experienced romantic relationships motivated by physical attraction alone, inner beauty relegated to the background. Sometimes, when I was asked to pray to know the will of God about my future wife, I turned to mockery: I myself could make the right choice without referring to God. Why bother God Eternal with something that I could handle on my own?

Since the events of Cotonou and Abidjan, I had matured. I had understood that God should be first in my life, the center of everything,[81] that I had to listen to his will, including the key issue of the choice of my spouse. Moreover, in my letter in Abidjan, I had asked Him to lead me to the woman whom He had planned for me to marry.

With time, my friendship with Natasha grew. We developed a natural complicity. I valued the sincerity of her character, and her devotion to serve the Lord. Still, I

---

81   "Delight yourself also in the Lord,
     And He shall give you the desires of your heart." (Psalms 37:4)

did not consider anything more than friendship. Crossing the Rubicon towards a romantic relationship was out of the question. Nonetheless, I suspected that this young woman, who laughed so easily with me, would eventually fall in love. Later, when deeper feelings began to rise in me, I offered resistance. Did I prefer her as a friend? Was I still attracted to other young women? I had to decide, to make a choice. I had to follow my heart, but I did not really know what it wanted: Natasha was sweet, discreet and a natural beauty; the other girls dazzled me. This might have been the real reason I was procrastinating: these women with their glitz and cosmetics fascinated me.

God wanted to correct my attitude. After teaching me faith, perseverance, patience, sacrifice and humility, He was going to teach me obedience.[82] During my walks in nature in Nancy, I had promised Him obedience in all things. The time had come to prove it... The voice of God that I had learned to recognize was again made clear in my heart: God had chosen Natasha for me. So I had to obey Him.

I wish I had voluntarily chosen Natasha on my own — she had beautiful qualities — but God intervened to make me understand that I did not have a choice: I was not to compare her with any other woman. Why did God get so involved in this? Could He not leave me to my own judgment? I realized that God did not want to take the risk of letting me choose a woman who would undermine his plans for my life. He had invested too much in me to let me make a bad choice of partner. The chosen one had to have been prepared by the Lord himself, had to fit perfectly into his plan,[83] in agreement with the visions of Cotonou.

When I crossed the Rubicon in obedience to the will of God, I discovered a new Natasha, as if she had been

---

[82] "... Behold, to obey is better than sacrifice..." (1 Samuel 15:22)
[83] "For I know the thoughts that I think toward you, says the LORD, thoughts of peace and not of evil, to give you a future and a hope." (Jeremiah 29:11)

transformed, as if the true face of this young woman had been hidden from me all this time. Every day, God showed me a new side of her personality, of her beauty, of her feminine charm. In fact, any procrastinating was not justified because Natasha was a woman according to the desire of my heart, both in character and physical qualities. So, following my act of obedience, God had opened my eyes to reveal the precious pearl he has polished for me. I understood that God knew the desires of my heart better than I did myself. He had presented to me the woman whom I had asked Him for in my letter in Abidjan: beautiful and virtuous.[84]

Driving me to the airport on July 3, 2012, Natasha knew that she would not see me for a long time: I was going to live far away from France. It was a painful separation, but I would also prepare a place for her in a country she had always admired. Our wedding was planned for a year later; during that reasonable delay, I would have time to establish myself in this new country in anticipation of the arrival of my future wife. So I was eager to leave France, where I had lived for two years; I was looking forward to a new challenge, to a new adventure with God. But still, we had to get to the airport on time.

We were still lost in Paris, not knowing which highway would get us to Roissy-Charles-de-Gaulle. The tension was thickening in the car. I now needed a miracle to make it to the airport on time... and the miracle happened! We asked for directions to another driver. Fortunately for us, the driver did not merely give us directions, he offered to take us there. He abandoned his original route, and took the road towards the airport. Natasha and I followed. Thus hope was reborn, and I made it on time for my flight.

The trip was going to be very long. The first leg of my trip was from Paris to Frankfurt, Germany, then from

---

[84] "He who finds a wife finds a good thing,
And obtains favor from the LORD." (Proverbs 18:22)

Frankfurt to Las Vegas, and, finally, I had a last connection from Las Vegas to Seattle. I was going to live in the United States as a permanent resident, a status obtained through my participation in the *American lottery*.

In October 2010, I had participated in the American lottery for the fifth time. The previous times I had not been selected. The federal government of the United States admits only 50,000 people each year through this program. However, millions of people participate worldwide. The American lottery is a program developed by the U.S. government to help underrepresented populations in the country to immigrate, a unique opportunity to access the American dream, except that, by definition, the selection process is random. Because many people meet the selection criteria, a computer randomly selects the lucky ones. In general, the winners of the lottery are announced in May, and then whoever is selected needs a full year to complete the entire procedure before flying to the United States.

The year 2010 had been my year of blessings. God had heard my request made in my letter in Abidjan in April of the same year. Something extraordinary had happened during the selection process; God had to be behind it. The winners of the 2010 lottery had been announced in May 2011. Unfortunately, I was not on the list. Then, a dramatic turn of events! A few days after having announced the 2011 winners, the U.S. agency responsible for the management of the lottery disclosed that an error had occurred in the selection process. To choose the winners, the computer had included only the applications submitted at the beginning of October 2010. It had not recognized all those who had submitted their application at the end of October. I was in that group. Seeing this computer error, the U.S. agency had decided to redo the selection. The new results would appear two months later.

The Fullness of the Blessing

On July 16, 2011, at around 2 A.M., I arrived home exhausted after a hard day's work at my place of internship and at the restaurant. I connected to the Internet, and navigated to the American lottery site... What I read made me burst into tears: « Dear ANTOINE DESIRE ONGOLO, you are among those randomly selected for further processing in the Diversity Immigrant Visa Program for the fiscal year 2012." I had won the American *green card*. If anything, the Lord was behind the second drawing, only so that I would be among the winners. I was the subject of a real miracle!

In Frankfurt, I had to get into another plane for Las Vegas. Once on board, I began to look for my seat number in the *economy class*. As I could not find it, a hostess approached me, looked at my boarding pass, and then pointed to the *business class*. I was hesitant. I wanted to tell her that I had paid for *economy class*, but she told me that my place was in *business class*. So I took my seat in the first row of the *business class*, just behind the *first class*. Definitely, I was the son of the living God, who sits the poor at the table of the rich. My neighbor looked at my boarding pass, and noted that I was not supposed to be in *business class*. "You're lucky," he said. But it was not luck; it was God's favor.

His favor accompanied me all the way to the United States. At the airport in Las Vegas, I met a boy of about sixteen who was on the same flight with me. He, too, had a connection flight to Seattle, where his mother was waiting. When we were given our new boarding passes for this flight within the United States, I discovered that my seat was right next to that of the young man with whom I had struck a friendship earlier. Therefore, I knew that God was preparing another surprise for me...

Upon our arrival in Seattle on the evening of July 3, 2012, my new friend's mother was waiting for him. I searched for my friend Yanick, who was supposed to pick me up. I looked for him for nearly half an hour, in vain. The family of the teenager had waited for me all this time. The boy's mother did not want to leave me stranded. And as God had foreseen everything, that American woman spoke perfect French: she had lived in Belgium in the past. Communication, therefore, was very easy between us.

As Yanick was not showing up, the lady offered to take me home. We took the road towards the city of Redmond, where Yanick was living. After traveling in business class, I was driven home by a stranger, like a king. My American adventure could not have a better start: God Himself was guiding me.

On the way to Redmond, I could not help but look everywhere: the scenery was gorgeous! I was discovering that a vast forest of fir trees, dotted with several lakes, surrounds Seattle. I was just realizing how deeply "Psalm 23" had touched my life: "... He makes me to lie down in green pastures; He leads me beside the still waters. ..."

Later, Yanick found me on the ground floor of his apartment building, visibly perplexed. He did not understand how we could have missed each other at the airport. Indeed, he had been at the arrival of my flight and had looked for me, everywhere. Inside, I knew that God was at work again: He had not wanted Yanick take me home. Had it been the case, I could have put my trust in this young man, who was somehow my sponsor in the United States. By having a stranger drive me home, God wanted to show me that He was guiding my destiny. He wanted to tell me that I should not rely on a man, but continue to depend on Him at the beginning of this new adventure...

"Jesus said to him, 'If you can believe, all things are possible to him who believes.'" Mark 9:23

The Fullness of the Blessing

First day in the United States, July 4, 2012.

First day in the United States, July 4, 2012.

A Letter to God

Antoine and Laure's (Natasha) wedding in Paris, July 2013.

The Fullness of the Blessing

Antoine and Laure's (Natasha) wedding in Paris, July 2013".

Epilogue

Everyone has a story. You have just read mine! It was written in pain, as you have noticed, but in hindsight, I am glad I have lived these moments of great suffering. Indeed, were it not for these hardships, I probably would not have a story to tell. The Bible teaches us that all things work together for good to those who love God. From my journey through the desert, a book has emerged, and I am proud of it. I hope it has strengthened your faith in God. Yes, every Christian should expect to go through hard times, but whatever the intensity of your grief, know that God is faithful and does not abandon us. Persevere and put your trust in God, for without faith, no one can please Him. Surely, the Lord can fulfill your needs. So, do not be discouraged, because soon your test trial will be your testimony.

If you have not yet had the opportunity to make Jesus Christ your Lord and Savior, or if, for some reason or another, you turned your back to the Christian life, I would like to give you the opportunity to reconcile with God by his son Jesus Christ. The Bible says that Jesus Christ is the way, the truth and the life, and that no one comes to the Father except through Him. He took upon Himself the punishment that was reserved for our sins. By his wounds, we are saved. The price has already been paid, you simply have to accept the sacrifice of Jesus Christ on the cross, and invite Him into your life as your Lord and personal Savior. Then you will inherit eternal life. Wherever you are, say the following prayer aloud:

"Lord Jesus, I acknowledge that I am a sinner. I ask you to forgive me all the sins I have committed in thought, word and deed. I acknowledge that you are the Son of God, and that you gave your life on the cross at Calvary to save me. I accept this sacrifice, and receive you into my life as my personal Lord and Savior. Fill me with your Holy Spirit now, and make me the person you want me to be. In the name of Jesus Christ. Amen!"

If you have prayed this prayer with a sincere heart, you have become a child of God, old things have passed away, and all things have become new. As a newborn, you will need a guide in your new life with Christ. This will involve beginning to attend church in order to grow spiritually. I am confident that the same God who has led me from Africa to the United States will lead you to the church he had planned especially for you. Ask the Holy Spirit to guide your steps, and you will be amazed.

I would appreciate it if you would communicate your impressions, comments and suggestions to me after you have read this book. You may send me a message at the following email address:
alettertogodstory@gmail.com

May the Lord bless you abundantly!

Antoine D. Ongolo